The Royal Commission on
Historical Manuscripts

Accessions to Repositories
and Reports added to the
National Register of Archives

1991

London: HMSO

ISBN 0 11 440229 9

ISSN 0308-0986

Printed in the United Kingdom for HMSO
Dd 293662 8/92 C7

Preface

Accessions to Repositories sets out to provide a concise report of the more important or unusual accessions to record repositories in the British Isles during the past year. Further information about these and about their routine accessions should be sought from the repositories themselves.

The Commission is again grateful to all those who have responded to its annual request for information. In response to suggestions from several contributing repositories for the first time this year entries include the repository accession numbers or references where this information was available. In addition to their publication here brief details from the returns are entered in the indexes of the National Register of Archives until these references can be superseded by fuller lists.

Contributions from over 200 repositories have been included in Part I of this year's issue, which has been edited for press by Mary Ellis assisted by Chris Evans, Rosemary Hayes, Kevin Morgan, Alex Ritchie and Jonathan Spain. Part II contains the usual list of numbered reports added to the National Register of Archives during the year, as well as some of the more interesting additions to and replacements of existing reports.

CJ KITCHING
Secretary

Quality House, Quality Court,
Chancery Lane, London WC2A 1HP

Contents

Note on access

The inclusion of material in Part I of this
publication does not necessarily imply
that it is yet available for research.
Enquiries about access should in all cases
be directed to the relevant repositories.

I: Accessions to Repositories

National and Special Repositories

ABERDEEN UNIVERSITY

DEPARTMENT OF SPECIAL
COLLECTIONS AND ARCHIVES,
UNIVERSITY LIBRARY, KING'S
COLLEGE, ABERDEEN AB9 2UB

Burnett family, baronets, of Leys:
family and estate papers 16th–18th cent
(MS 3361)

George Mackenzie Dunnet, professor of
zoology: papers c1950–80 (MS 3365)

A Strath-Maxwell, genealogist: collected
deeds rel to the North-East of Scotland
16th–17th cent (MS 3366)

BIRMINGHAM UNIVERSITY

UNIVERSITY LIBRARY, SPECIAL
COLLECTIONS DEPARTMENT,
EDGBASTON, BIRMINGHAM B15 2TT

Wilks family of Dudley: papers incl
corresp 17th–19th cent

Church Pastoral-Aid Society records
c1834–1950

Matacong Islands, West Africa (addnl):
records rel to territorial dispute 19th
cent

BRISTOL UNIVERSITY

UNIVERSITY LIBRARY, TYNDALL
AVENUE, BRISTOL BS8 1TJ

Goldney family of Clifton: deeds,
corresp and papers 18th–19th cent
(DM 1398)

Liberal Party, Yorkshire: records
1979–88 (DM 1411)

BRITISH ARCHITECTURAL LIBRARY

ROYAL INSTITUTE OF BRITISH
ARCHITECTS, 66 PORTLAND PLACE,
LONDON W1N 4AD

Joseph Bonomi (addnl): design drawings
(155) for various houses incl Rosneath,
Dunbartonshire c1782–1806
(Acc/1991.40)

Alec Clifton-Taylor, architectural
historian and critic: notebooks 1953–73
(Acc/M297)

Thomas Hardwick (addnl): sketchbooks
(3) of topographical drawings of Rome
1776–77 (Acc/1991.17)

John Harper: designs (17) for villas and
cottages c1830 (Acc/1991.4)

Hoar, Marlow & Lovett, Westminster:
design drawings (113) for Gatwick
Airport 'Beehive Building' 1935–36
(Acc/1991.28)

Dennis Lennon & Partners,
Westminster: design and working
drawings incl schemes for the interior
of the liner *Queen Elizabeth II* 20th cent
(Acc/1991.35)

James Leoni: design drawings (14) for
21 Arlington Street, London 1738
(Acc/1991.21)

Stephen Wright: design for the grotto
at Oaklands Park, Surrey 1765
(Acc/1991.8)

BRITISH LIBRARY

MANUSCRIPT COLLECTIONS,
GREAT RUSSELL STREET,
LONDON WC1B 3DG

Byron family, Barons Byron: corresp
and papers *c*1830–1940 (Dep 9004)

Lady Diana Cooper (addnl): corresp
*c*1908–17 (Add MSS 70704–20)

Sir Edward Dering MP, 2nd Bt (addnl):
household book 1652–85
(Add MS 70887)

Nathan Drake: journal of the siege of
Pontefract Castle 1644–45
(Add MS 70829)

Christabel Mary McLaren, Lady
Aberconway (addnl): corresp 1911–71
(Add MSS 70775–79, 70831–70838)

Evelyn Waugh, novelist: corresp
1921–66 (Dep 8873)

Virginia Woolf, novelist and critic
(addnl): *Hyde Park Gate News* 1891–92,
1895 (Add MSS 70725–26)

Lord Chamberlain's Office: corresp rel
to licensing of plays 1900–68
(Dep 8948)

Draft biography of William Pitt
(1759–1806), thought to be by George
Pretyman Tomline 1789
(Add MS 70827)

*Photographic copies of exported MSS
acquired through the Department of Trade
under the Export Licensing Regulations and
which became available for use during 1990
include the following:*

Henry Edward Manning, cardinal:
letters (41) mainly to his brother
1847–92 (RP 2824)

John Henry Newman, cardinal: letters
(35) 1855–75 (RP 2708 and 2752)

Lady Mary Powell of Pengethley,
Herefordshire: corresp (*c*40 items) rel to
Somerset estates 1629–32 (RP 2860 D–F)

ORIENTAL AND INDIA OFFICE
COLLECTIONS, 197 BLACKFRIARS
ROAD, LONDON SE1 8NG

Charles Milner Ricketts, member of the
Supreme Council of India: corresp
1817–18 (Mss Eur D 1234)

Arthur Herbert Cocks, Bengal Civil
Service: diaries and letters *c*1837–63
(Mss Eur F 240)

William Selby Taylor, plantation
superintendent, Ceylon: album of letters
and drawings 1844–50 (Mss Eur D 1221)

John Blomefield, chaplain to the bishop of
Calcutta, and his wife Sophia Elizabeth:
letters 1850–56 (Mss Eur C 541)

Herbert William Waite, Indian Police:
diaries, letters, casebooks and
photographs 1913–67 (Mss Eur D 1233)

Archibald Hyndman Stein, Indian
Forest Service: papers and photographs
*c*1923–63 (Mss Eur G 121)

Donald Langham Scott, postmaster in
India: letters 1925–37 (Mss Eur D 1232)

Freeman Freeman-Thomas, 1st
Marquess of Willington: letters as
governor-general of Canada and viceroy
of India 1926–36 (Mss Eur F 237)

Herbert Fagent Merrington, Indian
Service of Engineers, and his wife
Gillian Mary Elizabeth: letters 1927–41
(Mss Eur D 1229)

Coopers Hill Society: collected papers rel to the Royal Indian Engineering College, Coopers Hill 1872–1961 (Mss Eur F 239)

CAMBRIDGE UNIVERSITY

DEPARTMENT OF MANUSCRIPTS, UNIVERSITY LIBRARY, WEST ROAD, CAMBRIDGE CB3 9DR

Medingen Priory of Cistercian nuns, Verden diocese: order book 14th cent (Add MS 8850)

Syon Abbey: processional of Bridgettine use c1460–80 (Add MS 8885)

College of Cardinals, Rome: copies of letters to and from cardinals 1540–1669, compiled late 17th cent (Add MS 8852)

Langham family, baronets, of Cottesbrooke: genealogical notes 17th–18th cent (Add MS 8845)

George Hull Bowers (1794–1872), dean of Manchester: corresp and papers (Add MS 8862)

Edward John Mostyn Bowlby (1907–90), psychiatrist: corresp and notes rel to his biography of Charles Darwin (Add MS 8884)

John Clerke and Richard Blakewall: readings in Clement's Inn 1543–44 (Add MS 8871)

Sir Charles Louis des Graz (1860–1940), diplomat: letters to his mother (Add MS 8883)

Vice-Admiral Robert Fitzroy, hydrographer: letters, mainly to his family 1816–52 (Add MS 8853)

Robert Gardner, fellow of Emmanuel College: lecture notes and papers for the classical tripos 1908–55 (Add MS 8859)

Leonard Hugh Graham Greenwood, fellow of Emmanuel College: lecture notes and essays for the classical tripos 1910–58 (Add MS 8860)

John Jeffrey, fellow of Pembroke College: sermons preached at Holy Trinity Church 1619 (Add MS 8854)

William Arnold de Gorges Lloyd, educationalist: papers on education in South Africa c1950–70 (Add MS 8882)

Thaddeus Robert Rudolph Mann, biochemist: notebooks on the physiology and biochemistry of reproduction 1947–76 (Add MS 8880)

George Edward Moore, philosopher (addnl): lecture notes and papers 1895–1933 (Add MS 8875)

Alfred Rose (1840–1919), fellow of Emmanuel College: theological lectures (Add MS 8858)

Redcliffe Nathan Salaman (1874–1955), physiologist (addnl): scientific and personal papers (Add MS 8171)

George Skinner (c1796–1871), fellow of Jesus College: corresp (Add MS 8856)

Miles and Henry Stapylton, clergymen: commonplace books and papers c1677–1745 (Add MS 8861)

John Stuart, 3rd Earl of Bute, prime minister: travel writings c1768–87 (Add MS 8826)

Sir William Trumbull (1639–1716), secretary of state: papers and collections rel to Oxford University, his embassy to France, his legal career, and Spanish history (Add MSS 8863–68)

John Symonds Udal, Attorney General of Fiji and Chief Justice of the Leeward Islands: letters to him on genealogy, antiquarian subjects and folklore 1877–1916 (Add MS 8855)

Alexander Stuart Watt (1892–1985), plant ecologist: botanical notebooks and papers (Add MS 8851)

Treatise defending Sir Isaac Newton against attack by George Gordon, possibly by George Pirrie, early 18th cent (Add MS 8874)

Cambridge University Swimming Club (addnl): records 1912–76 (Add MS 8088)

UNIVERSITY ARCHIVES

Cambridge University Press (addnl): draft proposal and letters of Lord Acton rel to the *Cambridge Modern History* 1896–1901

Wolfson College: corresp and papers rel to foundation and statutes 1962–77

CHURCHILL ARCHIVES CENTRE,
CHURCHILL COLLEGE,
CAMBRIDGE CB3 0DS

Albert Victor Alexander, 1st Earl Alexander of Hillsborough, politician (addnl): papers 1940–60 (AVAR)

Major PG Hampton, Royal Artillery: memoirs of service in France and Belgium 1940–44 (HPTN)

Sydney Jones, railway engineer: papers rel to the conformable wheel 1965–90 (JNES)

John Ashworth Ratcliffe (1902–87), physicist (addnl): corresp and papers (RACL)

John Seddon (1915–91), aeronautical engineer: papers (SDDN)

Admiral Sir Arthur Francis Turner (1912–91), naval engineer: corresp and papers (TRNR)

Channel Tunnel Association (addnl): papers c1980–89 (CTUN)

MODERN ARCHIVE CENTRE,
KING'S COLLEGE,
CAMBRIDGE CB2 1ST

Oscar Browning (1837–1923), educational reformer and historian (addnl): papers (OB)

John Davy Hayward, anthologist and bibliophile (addnl): letters 1955–56 (JDH)

Sir Charles Otto Desmond MacCarthy, author and literary critic (addnl): letters 1936–50 (MISC)

Gerald Frank Shove, economist: letters 1911–12 (MISC)

'Bloomsbury Group' Play Reading Society: minute book 1907–15 (CHAO)

Society of the Caroline Club: minute book 1914–15 (MISC)

TRINITY COLLEGE LIBRARY,
CAMBRIDGE CB2 1TQ

Sir Dennis Holme Robertson (1890–1963), political economist: corresp and papers

Ludwig Wittgenstein, philosopher (addnl): papers, and letters to GR Pattison c1930–39

CHURCH OF ENGLAND
RECORD CENTRE

15 GALLEYWALL ROAD,
SOUTH BERMONDSEY,
LONDON SE16 3PB

St Audries School, West Quantoxhead, Somerset: records 1906–91 (NS/SR/STA, NS/STA)

CHURCH OF IRELAND

REPRESENTATIVE CHURCH BODY
LIBRARY, BRAEMOR PARK,
RATHGAR, DUBLIN 14

Lord John George de la Poer Beresford, archbishop of Armagh (addnl): corresp 1820–62 (MS 513) (partly transferred from Meath Diocesan Registry)

Christ Church Cathedral, Dublin (addnl): records 1710–1978 (C.6)

Meath diocese records 18th–20th cent (D.7)

Meath Protestant Orphan Society: records incl minutes and accounts 1844–1986 (MS 312)

Merchant Tailors Endowments, Dublin: records incl Dublin Guild of Tailors 1642–1963 (MS 338)

DUBLIN UNIVERSITY

TRINITY COLLEGE LIBRARY,
COLLEGE STREET, DUBLIN 2

Dillon family (addnl): papers, mainly rel to the family business, Monica Duff & Co Ltd, Ballaghaderreen 19th–20th cent (MSS 10540–2)

Ware family of Dublin: household book 1728–81 (MS 10528)

Liam de Roiste (1882–1959), Sinn Fein MP and lecturer: corresp and papers (MS 10539)

William Monck Mason (1775–1859), historian (addnl): MS history of Christ Church Cathedral, Dublin (MSS 10529–30)

Susan L Mitchell (1866–1926), author: papers (MS 10543)

DUNDEE UNIVERSITY

UNIVERSITY LIBRARY, ARCHIVES
AND MANUSCRIPTS DEPARTMENT,
DUNDEE DD1 4HN

Don Brothers, Buist & Co Ltd, flax and jute spinners and mfrs, Dundee (addnl): records 1875–1964 (MS 100)

Douglas & Grant Ltd, engineers and mill wrights, Dunnikier foundry, Kirkcaldy (addnl): sketch books 1903–26 (MS 45)

Tayside Health Board: minutes of Angus, Perth and Kinross, and Dundee health insurance committees and National Health Service executive council committees 1912–74; and Eastern Joint Ophthalmic Services committee 1948–74 (Acc M/274)

DURHAM UNIVERSITY

UNIVERSITY LIBRARY, ARCHIVES
AND SPECIAL COLLECTIONS,
PALACE GREEN SECTION,
PALACE GREEN,
DURHAM DH1 3RN

Old Park, Wolsingham: estate plan 1725 (Acc SC 1990/91:2)

Thomas Hodgkin (1831–1913), historian: MS translation of the letters of Cassiodorus (Acc SC 1990/91:5)

Sudan Archive

Brigadier Peter Bevil Edward Acland (addnl): papers rel to his Sudan service 1925–46 and memoir by his wife (Acc SAD G//S 999)

Oliver Claude Allison, bishop of the Sudan: papers incl material rel to Anglican missionary activity in southern Sudan c1905–20 (Acc SAD G//S 1013)

Lt-Colonel S Austin: diary and memoir describing his journey to the Bahr-al-Ghazal 1916 and service in Kafia Kingi (Acc SAD G//S 984)

Olive A Gray: papers rel to her work for the Church Missionary Society in southern Sudan c1957–65 (Acc SAD G//S 1008)

Winifred Johnson: diaries rel to her life in the Gezira, central Sudan 1946–53 (Acc SAD G//S 994)

JGS Macphail (addnl): papers, mainly rel to the Upper Nile Province 1923–47 (Acc SAD G//S 991)

THB Mynors: papers incl material on the Moru tribe and southern Sudan 1930–55 (Acc SAD G//S 988)

Charles H Smith, director of the Sudan Gezira Board: papers c1950–59 (Acc SAD G//S 1012)

John Oliver Udal: papers, mainly rel to the Shilluk tribe 1950–55 (Acc SAD G//S 989)

Nicholas Robin Udal (1883–1964) (addnl): papers concerning his work for the Sudan Education Department and as warden of Gordon College, Khartoum (Acc SAD G//S 989)

J Winder (addnl): papers incl MS 'A picture of life in the Upper Nile Province' 1927–55 (Acc SAD G//S 995)

Hayton, Lee & Braddock, architects,
Durham: papers rel to work as
architects to the diocese of Durham
1935–89 (HLB papers)

EDINBURGH UNIVERSITY

Thomas Carlyle, essayist and historian
(addnl): letters (8) 1854–70

Walter de la Mare, poet (addnl): letters
(50) and papers 1921–52

John Middleton Murry, author (addnl):
letters (20) and MS of *Heaven and Earth*

Sir Walter Scott, novelist and poet
(addnl): letters (5) 1814–30, and MS of
Helvellyn

FAWCETT LIBRARY

Dame Geraldine Maitland Aves
(1898–1986), public servant: corresp and
papers (7/GMA)

Mary Stott, journalist and feminist:
papers rel to her work with the
Townswomen's Guild c1950–79
(7/CMS)

St Joan's International Alliance, UK
section (addnl): records 1982–90 (5/SJI)

London Feminist History Group:
attendance book 1981–89 (5/LFH)

Blackfriars Settlement, formerly
Women's University Settlement:
records 1887–1974 (5/WUS)

GLASGOW UNIVERSITY

'A Diurnal of remarkable occurrents...
within Scotland' c1513–1575

Rudolf Schlesinger (1901–69), director
of the Institute of Soviet and Eastern
European Studies at Glasgow
University: papers

Sir David Paton Cuthbertson,
pathological biochemist:
autobiographical essays 1930–90
(DC 296)

Barr & Stroud Ltd, optical instrument
mfrs, Glasgow: records incl letter books
and ledgers 1893–1974 (UGD 295)

Chery & Sandford Properties, estate
agents, Glasgow: property books
1930–74 (UGD 300)

Coats Viyella plc, textile mfrs (addnl):
records of Scottish subsidiaries c1920–60
(UGD 199)

House of Fraser plc, department store,
Glasgow (addnl): head office salaries
books c1960–79 (HF)

Long John International Ltd, distillers,
Glasgow: minutes and financial records
incl subsidiaries c1700–1980 (UGD 306)

North British Locomotive Co Ltd and
Neilson, Reid & Co Ltd, locomotive
builders, Glasgow: plans c1870–1953
(transferred from the Mitchell Library,
Glasgow)

Scottish Northern Investment Trust plc:
ledgers c1960–79 (UGD 303)

Thomas Stewart & Son Ltd, plumbers,
Methil: records incl cash books 1940–65
(UGD 315)

Vulcan Foundry Ltd, locomotive builders, Newton-le-Willows: technical records 20th cent (UGD 314)

Whiteleys Farm, Cardross: records c1920–90 (UGD 313)

British Corporation for the Survey and Registry of Shipping: hull and machinery survey reports 1891–1949 (UGD 304)

Glasgow Chamber of Commerce: financial records c1920-65 (UGD 312)

HOUSE OF LORDS

RECORD OFFICE, HOUSE OF LORDS, LONDON SW1A 0PW

Warren Hastings, governor-general of India: notebooks (8) recording 7 days of his trial 1790–92 (in Gurney shorthand) (Historical Collection 367)

HULL UNIVERSITY

BRYNMOR JONES LIBRARY, THE UNIVERSITY, HULL HU6 7RX

Hotham family, Barons Hotham (addnl): estate papers 19th–20th cent (DDHO)

St Quintin family of Scampston (addnl): family and estate papers 18th–19th cent (DDSQ)

Philip Larkin (1922–85), poet: corresp and papers (DPL)

David Neave, historian: research material incl original records of East Yorkshire friendly societies c1800–1989 (DFR)

Beverley and Haltemprice Social Democratic Party records c1980–89 (DSD)

Campaign for Labour Party Democracy records 1973–91 (DX/222)

Beverley Minster 'Open Space' Campaign records c1980–89 (DBE)

IMPERIAL WAR MUSEUM

LAMBETH ROAD, LONDON SE1 6HZ

RJ Bailey, commercial artist: letters and drawings rel to service on the Western Front, Salonika and South Russia 1914–19

Captain Ronald Christopher Bayne: naval papers 1910–46

Wing Commander Guy M Brisbane: papers rel to service with Bomber Command incl participation in the *Scharnhorst* raid 1938–58

Air Commodore John Constable-Roberts: papers 1926–54

Captain WP Cliff: diaries of service in the 22nd Sam Browne's Cavalry, Mesopotamia 1916–19

Captain Richard Henry Courage: naval papers 1927–51

Major-General Eric Victor Howard Fairtlough: letters and papers 1907–44

Air Vice-Marshal James Richmond Gordon-Finlayson: pilot's log book of service with Bomber Command in North Africa, Europe, India and South East Asia 1940–47

General Sir James Michael Gow: letters rel to service in North West Europe as a lieutenant in the Scots Guards 1944–45

Major-General Sir Henry West Hodgson: letters rel to his commands in Gallipoli, Egypt and Palestine 1915–19

Rear-Admiral Christopher Haynes Hutchinson: papers 1919–62

Captain Stanley Brian de Courcy Ireland: naval memoirs 1913–51

Captain HW Luttman-Johnson: diary, letters and papers rel to his secretaryship of the January and Windsor clubs c1930–39, and his detention during World War II

Engineer Rear-Admiral Geoffrey J
Morgan: diaries of service in the
Mediterranean and North West Europe
1940–45

Lt-General Edmund Archibald Osborne:
diary and papers rel to service as GOC
44th Division incl the evacuation of
Dunkirk 1940–41

Sir Robert Parr, diplomat: papers rel to
service in the Serbian army and with
the British military mission 1914–18

Major Sir Harold Alwyne Pelly, 5th Bt
(addnl): papers 1943–49

Admiral of the Fleet Sir Alfred Dudley
Pickman Rogers Pound: diary of service
in HMS *St Vincent* 1914–15

General Sir Montagu George North
Stopford (addnl): diaries 1932–35

Air Marshal Stephen Charles Strafford:
diaries, letters and papers rel to service
with the RNAS and RAF during the
world wars

Vice-Admiral Sir George Thomas
Carlisle Parker Swabey: memoirs
1895–1945

Major John H Wagstaff: narrative of
his escape from Singapore 1942

INSTITUTION OF CIVIL ENGINEERS

1-7 GREAT GEORGE STREET,
LONDON SW1P 3AA

James Cooper, civil engineer: journal rel
to his work in James Walker's office
1833–41

John Dixon: notebook rel to London-
Brighton Railway incl notes for
evidence to parliamentary committee
1836

Engineers notebook rel to railways in
the North East of England 1829–30

INSTITUTION OF ELECTRICAL ENGINEERS

SAVOY PLACE, LONDON WC2R 0BL

Leslie Herbert Bedford, president of the
Institution of Electronic and Radio
Engineers: research notebooks 1949–81

IRONBRIDGE GORGE MUSEUM

TELFORD, SHROPSHIRE TF8 7AW

William Southorn & Co, clay tobacco
pipe mfrs, Broseley: records incl those
of Rowland Smitheman & Co
1860–1960

Kenyon-Slaney family of Hatton
Grange: leases and plans rel to
Coalbrookdale coalfield and agreements
with the Darby family 1817–95

LAMBETH PALACE LIBRARY

LONDON SE1 7JU

Book of Hours, Use of Sarum (English)
*c*1280–90

Lancelot Mason, archdeacon of
Chichester: corresp and papers 1922–58

William Sancroft, archbishop of
Canterbury: letters (37) to William
Lloyd, bishop of Norwich, 1680–92

Frederick James Western, bishop of
Tinnevelly, India: ecumenical papers
1933–45

Churches Council on Alcohol and
Drugs records 20th cent

United Kingdom Band of Hope Union
records 19th–20th cent

Survey of offices in crown patronage
*c*1610–12

LEEDS UNIVERSITY

BROTHERTON LIBRARY,
UNIVERSITY OF LEEDS, LEEDS LS2 9JT

Maurice Warwick Beresford (b1920), historian: corresp and papers (910)

Jack Eric Morpurgo, professor of American literature (addnl): corresp and papers 1971–78 (963)

Esther Simpson: corresp and papers, mainly as secretary of the Society for the Protection of Science and Learning 1918–91 (959)

Association for Science Education (addnl): records c1926–75 (MS Dep 1991/3)

Brotherton Collection

John Gibson (1630–1711), of Welburn: transcripts of poems by Andrew Marvell, Edmund Waller, John Wilmot, 2nd Earl of Rochester and others (MS Lt.q 52)

Liddle Collection, Edward Boyle Library

Norman Gaudie, conscientious objector sentenced to death in 1916: corresp and papers

Guy Maynard Liddell (1892–1958), public servant: World War I photograph and sketch albums

HH McWilliam, naval prisoner of war: World War I diaries and paintings

Colonel Geoffrey Francis Phillips (1880–1968): East African campaign diaries

Admiral Sir Morgan Singer (1864–1938): corresp and account of his work as Director of Naval Ordnance during World War I

LIVERPOOL UNIVERSITY

ARCHIVES UNIT, PO BOX 147,
LIVERPOOL L69 3BX

Charles John Allen (1862–1936), sculptor: papers (D556)

Alan W Beeston (d1986), Pro-Chancellor, University of Liverpool: papers (D555)

Percy Maude Roxby, geographer (addnl): notes for lectures 1928–47 (D571)

Merseyside Conference for Overseas Students records 1961–87 (D557)

University of Liverpool Athletic Union (addnl): records 1926–91 (A104)

LONDON UNIVERSITY

UNIVERSITY OF LONDON LIBRARY,
SENATE HOUSE, MALET STREET,
LONDON WC1E 7HU

Laurie Gardiner (d1991), Tudor historian: papers (ULL MS 918)

Sylvia Legge, author: literary papers rel to the family life of Thomas Sturge Moore (1870–1944), writer and wood engraver (ULL MS 916)

BRITISH LIBRARY OF POLITICAL
AND ECONOMIC SCIENCE,
MANUSCRIPT DIVISION,
10 PORTUGAL STREET,
LONDON WC2A 2HD

Brian Abel-Smith, professor of social administration: papers c1970–89 (ABEL-SMITH)

Sir Sidney Caine (1902–90), director of the London School of Economics: papers incl rel to the early history of the LSE (CAINE)

Harold Cecil Edey, professor of accounting: papers c1950–79 (EDEY)

Sir Geoffrey Finsberg MP: political and constituency papers c1970–89 (FINSBERG)

Hugh Gater Jenkins, Baron Jenkins of Putney, politician: papers c1945–79 (JENKINS)

John Leonard Nicholson, chief economic adviser to the Department of Health and Social Security: papers c1950–89 (JLN)

Sir Cyril Philips: papers as chairman of the Royal Commission on Criminal Procedure 1978–84 (RCCP)

Anthony Fortescue Heyden Redman: papers rel to anti-EEC organisations incl the Anti-Common Market League c1972–84 (COLL MISC 763)

Derek Senior, writer: papers rel to town planning and local government c1940–88 (SENIOR)

Federal Union and Federal Trust for Education and Research: records c1938–89 (partly transferred from Sussex University Library) (FEDERAL TRUST)

College of Preceptors: council and committee minutes, examination and conference papers 1848–1945

Universities Council for the Education of Teachers: records 1967–78

Ronald Harry Graveson (1911–91), professor of private international law: papers

George MacDonald (1824–1905), poet and novelist: poems and corresp

Centre for Physiotherapy Research: papers from a national survey of electrotherapy research 1986–89

Colonel SC Aston: papers rel to the capture of Madagascar 1942

General Sir John Theodosius Burnett-Stuart (addnl): papers rel to the Moplah rebellion in India 1921–22, and army training exercises c1930–39

Major-General JB Churcher: memoirs rel to his command of 159 Infantry Brigade 1944–46

General Sir Beauvoir de Lisle: papers incl memoirs rel to the Egyptian campaign 1885–86, the Boer War 1899–1902, and World War I

WAC Haines, Malayan Police: memoir of his career 1920–50

Frank Harrison, wireless operator, 2nd Armoured Division: memoirs rel to the siege of Tobruk 1941

Lt-Colonel JAE Heard: papers rel to his work as head of the counter-propaganda service directed at Indian Army troops 1939–46

Captain Patrick O'Regan (addnl): corresp and papers rel to war service in France and Northern Italy 1943–45

Lt-Colonel Walter Temple Willcox: diaries and papers rel to his service with the 5th Royal Irish Lancers and the 3rd Kings Own Hussars in India, South Africa and Europe 1894–1920

Eric Blair, 'George Orwell', writer (addnl): corresp and papers incl diary 1947–48, corresp with his publishers 1945–47, and diary of his mother Ida Blair 1905 (Accs A 533–34)

Charles Kay Ogden, linguistic psychologist (addnl): papers and corresp with William Francis Jackson Knight rel to classical subjects c1940–50 (Acc A 532)

Egon Sharpe Pearson, statistician (addnl): corresp with David John Finney 1956–80 (MS ADD 380)

Sir George Dancer Thane, anatomist (addnl): notebook 1923–29 (MS ADD 282)

University College London Old Students' Association (addnl): minutes 1946–78 (Acc A 528)

MANCHESTER UNIVERSITY

METHODIST ARCHIVES AND
RESEARCH CENTRE,
MANCHESTER M3 3EH

Armed Services Board (Chaplaincy), Division of Ministries, and Division of Social Responsibility: records c1834–1991 (MA 6001)

NATIONAL ARCHIVES OF IRELAND

FOUR COURTS, DUBLIN 7

Palmer family, baronets, of Castle Lackin (addnl): estate papers 1670–1937 (Acc 1174)

Pim family, co Leix and co Wicklow: papers 17th–20th cent (Acc 1176)

John Errington, jesuit: papers 1847–1925 (Acc 1173)

James Adam & Sons, auctioneers and valuers, Dublin: records 20th cent (DUB 120)

Convoy Woollen Co Ltd: records incl minutes, accounts and wages books 1883–1987 (DON 27)

Morrin & Son Ltd, millers, Baltinglass: corresp, accounts and memorandum books 1850–1982 (WICK 30)

Odlum Group Ltd, millers, Dublin: records of mills and bakeries in Dublin and Sligo 1881–1991 (DUB 128)

R Perry & Co Ltd, ship chandlers, Dun Laoghaire: accounts and quotation books 1911–78 (DUB 126)

Shannon Industries Ltd, toy and giftware mfrs, Carrick-on-Shannon: corresp, accounts and wages books 20th cent (LEIT 5)

Eblana Loan and Investment Society, Dublin: corresp, accounts and rule books 1877–1934 (DUB 96)

Waterford Harbour Commissioners: minutes, letter books, accounts and plans 1816–1991 (WAT 8)

St Columba's Hospital, Sligo: minutes, admission registers, case books 1855–1985 (Acc 1184)

Records incl minutes of North Dublin, South Dublin and Balrothery poor law unions, rural district councils and boards of public assistance 1841–1950 (BG40, BG78–79)

NATIONAL ARMY MUSEUM

ROYAL HOSPITAL ROAD, CHELSEA,
LONDON SW3 4HT

Field Marshal George Townshend, 1st Marquess Townshend (addnl): letters (11) from Lt-General the hon Edward Cornwallis 1761–71 (9107–146)

Field Marshal Sir Stapleton Cotton, 1st Viscount Combermere: papers 1791–1865 (9104–21)

General Sir Eyre Coote (addnl): journal 1791 and misc papers 1797–1801 (9111–45)

Captain John Read Vincent, The King's Own Regiment: papers 1809–28 (9109–4)

Ensign Alexander Rose, 54th Bengal Native Infantry: 1st Afghan War letters (25) 1839–42 (9109–45)

Lt-Colonel George de Sausmarez, 21st Madras Native Infantry: letter book rel to rifle instruction 1857–59 (9109–3)

Leopold Poynder, chaplain at Calcutta: memoir of the outbreak of the Indian Mutiny at Bareilly 1857 (9101–39)

Lt-Colonel Cyril Godfrey Martyr, Duke of Cornwall's Light Infantry: Boer War diary and papers 1900–02 (9101–27)

S Vernon Robinson, surgeon: Boer War letters (23) 1900 (9101–20)

Roger John Kynaston Mott, secretary of the National Service League: corresp and papers incl letters from Lord Roberts 1909–14 (9101–96)

Lt-Colonel Robert George Browning, Indian Ordnance Corps: papers 1914–48 (9111–15)

Lt-Colonel John Mackillip Gordon: papers rel to 1st Bn, Queen's Own Cameron Highlanders 1915–16, and military prisons and punishment camps 1940–48 (9102–331)

Dr Alexander Frank Wallace: East African campaign letters (145) 1915–18 (9103–43)

Brigadier Sir Francis Smith Reid, secretary to the Speaker of the House of Commons: diaries and papers 1918–70 (9103–119)

Major Robert Francis Ruttledge, Poona Horse: hog-hunting journal 1922–34 (9103–27)

Lt-Colonel Christopher Ronald Spear, British military attache in Peking: corresp and papers rel to his arrest by the Japanese 1939 (9101–22)

Lt-Colonel Albert Geoffrey Miller: corresp rel to 112th Regt Royal Armoured Corps (Sherwood Foresters) 1941–44 (9107–234)

Captain Anthony D Roy, Royal Artillery: corresp and papers 1943–80 (9107–176)

Lt-Colonel William Alleyne Robinson: papers rel to establishment of Joint Services Staff College and Southern Cameroons plebiscite 1946–61 (9102–250, 9104–9)

Ministry of Defence files rel to the estates of soldiers who died in service 1902–60 (9102–333)

NATIONAL LIBRARY OF IRELAND

KILDARE STREET, DUBLIN 2

Edmund William Burton, father of the painter Samuel Frederick Burton: diaries 1804–08 (Ms.32, 485)

Richard Jones, 3rd Viscount and 1st Earl of Ranelagh, chancellor of the Irish exchequer: financial reports c1670–1710 (Acc 4563)

Pack-Beresford family of Fenagh, co Carlow: papers c1765–1830 (Acc 4584a)

Pakenham Mahon family of Strokestown, co Roscommon (addnl): family and estate papers c1760–1933 (Acc 4538)

NATIONAL LIBRARY OF SCOTLAND

DEPARTMENT OF MANUSCRIPTS, GEORGE IV BRIDGE, EDINBURGH EH1 1EW

Scott family, baronets, of Abbotsford: letters of family members to their governess 1813–37 (Acc 10401)

Skirving family of Haddington, East Lothian: corresp and papers c1780–1850 (Acc 10263)

Sir John Bisset, commissary-general in Spain: divisional letter book 1812 (Acc 10322)

Alan Bold, poet (addnl): corresp 1964–90 (Acc 10374)

George Mackay Brown, author (addnl): corresp 1974–87 (Acc 10372)

General Thomas Dalyell of Binns: report from Andrew Bruce of Earlshall on the battle of Airds Moss 1680 (Acc 10402)

Lt-General Sir Kenneth Douglas, 1st Bt: military corresp 1798–1811 (Acc 10458)

James Ferguson (1710–76), astronomer: corresp and papers (Acc 10254) (transferred from the Royal Society of Edinburgh)

Neil Gunn, author (addnl): corresp 1938–66 (Acc 10326)

Denys Hay, historian: radio scripts and research papers 1963–76 (Acc 10251)

Laurence Hill, solicitor (addnl): vol 1 of *Political State of Scotland* 1788–89 (Acc 10288)

Major-General Alastair Ian Macdougall: diary of war service 1914–18 (Acc 10430)

John Maitland, Duke of Lauderdale (1616–82): letters received mainly as secretary of state in Scotland (Acc 10442)

Robert Drysdale Smith, journalist: corresp 1914–18 (Acc 10295)

Sydney Goodsir Smith, poet (addnl): corresp and literary MSS 1923–74 (Accs 10281, 10397, 10426)

Robert Louis Stevenson, author: MS of *The History of Moses* 1856 (Acc 10356)

John Wilson, 'Christopher North' (1785–1854), author: corresp and papers (MSS 21240–41)

James Ballantyne & Co, printers, Edinburgh: trust and other papers rel to Sir Walter Scott's affairs 1824–33 (Acc 10270)

Aitken Dott & Son, fine art dealers, Edinburgh: records c1875–1955 (Acc 10421)

George Johnstone, bookseller, Dumfries: records 1810–16 (Acc 10262)

David & Charles Stevenson, civil engineers, Edinburgh (addnl): records 1752–1955 (Acc 10268)

Scottish Conservative and Unionist Association records 1870–1987 (Acc 10424)

Edinburgh Festival Guild records 1960–80 (Acc 10441)

NATIONAL LIBRARY OF WALES

DEPARTMENT OF MANUSCRIPTS AND RECORDS, ABERYSTWYTH SY23 3BU

Leo Abse (*b*1917) MP: papers

Euros Bowen (1904–88), poet: papers

Constance Bullock-Davies (*d*1989), lecturer: research papers rel to medieval history and literature

Lady Eleanor Butler (1739–1829), and Miss Sarah Ponsonby (1755–1831), 'The Ladies of Llangollen': letters (*c*70) to Mrs Margaret Wingfield of Rhiwabon (NLW MSS 22768D); and 'The Hamwood Papers' incl diaries, corresp and MSS

Lady Olwen Carey-Evans (1892–1990): family papers incl corresp of, and with her parents David and Margaret Lloyd George 1890–1942, and speech notes of David Lloyd George 1904–21

Idris Cox (1899–1989), Communist party activist in South Wales: papers incl unpublished autobiography

Rhys Davies (1903–78), novelist and short-story writer: personal and literary papers

James Hanley (1901–85), novelist (addnl): letters (*c*450) with Timmie Hanley mainly to their son

Cledwyn Hughes (*b*1919), Baron Cledwyn of Penrhos, politician: corresp and papers

John Barnard Jenkins, Welsh freedom movement activist: corresp and papers 1969–77 (NLW MSS 22816–19)

Ben G Jones (1914–89), Liberal politician, chairman of the Welsh Language Council and president of the Honourable Society of Cymmrodorion: papers

AG Prys-Jones (1888–1987), Anglo-Welsh writer: corresp and papers incl literary MSS

John Collwyn Rees (1919–80), professor of political theory and government at University College Swansea: research papers and corresp

William Leslie Richards (1916–89), poet and novelist: corresp and papers incl diaries

Albert James Sylvester, principal private secretary to David Lloyd George: corresp, shorthand diaries and transcriptions 1923–45

Jeffrey Thomas MP (1933–89): papers

Wynford Vaughan-Thomas (1908–87), author and broadcaster: papers incl war dispatches

NATIONAL MARITIME MUSEUM

MANUSCRIPTS SECTION,
GREENWICH, LONDON SE10 9NF

John Montagu, 4th Earl of Sandwich (addnl): papers c1738–92 (MS91/018)

John Ramsay, master: journals kept on voyages between England and Jamaica 1738–43 (MS91/023)

Donald Campbell, master: corresp and logs 1866–1914 (MS91/011)

Admiral Sir Edward Eden Bradford: papers 1867–1918 (MS91/012)

Rear-Admiral Royer Mylius Dick: papers c1914–50 (MS91/006)

Journal of a merchant seaman in the Mediterranean 1719–33 (MS91/026)

Union-Castle Line Ltd and Clan Line Steamers Ltd (addnl): records c1870–1978 (MS91/004)

Ship Builders and Ship Repairers Association: records 1977–90 (MS91/001)

NATIONAL MUSEUM OF LABOUR HISTORY

103 PRINCESS STREET,
MANCHESTER M1 6DD

Robert Edwards MP (1905–90): papers

Harry McShane, socialist: papers and corresp with Raya Dunayevskaya 1959–88

Labour Party (addnl): Parliamentary Labour Party minutes 1906–76; and European Parliament Labour Party records c1979–91

Chile Solidarity Campaign records 1973–91

NATIONAL MUSEUMS AND GALLERIES ON MERSEYSIDE

MERSEYSIDE MARITIME MUSEUM,
ALBERT DOCK, LIVERPOOL L3 4AA

WC Barker: letters, mainly from voyages to Australia and New Zealand 1856–76 (29/91)

W Baxter, ships engineer: papers 1920–80 (47/91)

Daniel Dow, master of the *Lusitania* and the *Mauretania*: papers 1907–20 (36/91)

GC Evans, master mariner: papers 1881–1923 (35/91)

FL Jordan, carpenter and boatswain: papers 1894–1927 (30/91)

W Paton, master of the *Great Eastern*: papers c1853–1937 (32/91)

Vernon Poole, ships surgeon: journal of West African voyage 1832–33 (27/91)

James Newton & Co Ltd, ship chandlers and sailmakers, Liverpool: records 1917–70 (22/91)

Liverpool Geological Society: minutes and papers 1859–1991 (52/91)

HMS *Conway*, school ship, Wallasey (addnl): records 1859–1970 (50/91)

THE NATURAL HISTORY MUSEUM

CROMWELL ROAD, LONDON SW7 5BD

Donovan Reginald Rosevear (1900–86), zoologist: diaries, corresp and photographs rel to mammalian research in Nigeria (BRN 90160)

Sir Charles Maurice Yonge (1899–1986), marine biologist: papers and corresp rel to research on the Great Barrier Reef (BRN 72360, BRN 93164)

John Codrington, botanist: notebooks (2) and botanical maps c1950–70 (BRN 89557, BRN 92908)

Christian Heuland, mineralogist: 'Catalogue de la collection des mineraux et cristallisations pierreuses de Monsieur de Clavijo' c1780 (BRN 92858)

Dawson Turner, botanist and antiquary (addnl): collected letters (31) of botanists 1777–1850 (BRN 92859)

Robert Henry F Rippon, entomologist: drawings (170) for *Icones Ornithopterorum* 1890–1910 (BRN 90301)

Janson & Sons, natural history dealers and booksellers, London: corresp, letter books and financial papers 1871–1927 (BRN 94325)

NOTTINGHAM UNIVERSITY

UNIVERSITY LIBRARY, MANUSCRIPTS DEPARTMENT, HALLWARD LIBRARY, UNIVERSITY PARK, NOTTINGHAM NG7 2RD

Maurice Willmore Barley (1909–91), archaeologist (addnl): papers (Acc 1123)

Eric Foster, Labour councillor: political papers c1970–79 (Acc 1117)

DH Lawrence (1885–1930), novelist and poet (addnl): literary papers (Accs 1054, 1097, 1124)

Frieda Lawrence, widow of DH Lawrence: corresp with Laurence Pollinger c1950–59 (Acc 1081)

Hilda Lewis (d1974), novelist (addnl): papers (Acc 1064)

Christopher J Wrigley, historian and local Labour politician: political papers c1980–89 (Acc 1090)

William Blake Bicentenary Celebration 1957: committee and related papers (Acc 1095)

OXFORD UNIVERSITY

DEPARTMENT OF WESTERN MANUSCRIPTS, BODLEIAN LIBRARY, OXFORD OX1 3BG

Walter Boothby: commonplace book c1632–65 (MS. Eng. c.2693)

Richard Chiswell MP, Turkey merchant: journals and notebooks 1696–1738 (MSS. Don. c.181–2, d.193–4, e.169)

John Parkinson (addnl): journals of northern tour 1792–93 (MSS. Eng. d.2296–7)

General Sir John Francis Caradoc, 1st Baron Howden, and Sir John Hobart Caradoc, 2nd Baron Howden: letter books 1806–58 (MSS. Eng. b.2028–32, c.2737–60, d.2294–5)

Karl Klingemann: letters to Felix Mendelssohn 1845–47

John Wodehouse, 1st Earl of Kimberley (1826–1902), stateman: political papers

Arthur Christopher Benson (1826–1925), Edward Frederic Benson (1867–1940), and Robert Hugh Benson (1871–1914), writers; Edward White Benson (1829–96), archbishop of Canterbury (addnl): corresp and literary papers

Philip Anthony Spalding, writer: diaries and papers 19th–20th cent (MSS. Eng. c.2763–802, d.2298–340, e.2433–607)

Aylwin Owen, printer: diaries 1918–50 (MSS. Eng e.2410–21)

John Stephen Hallett Clissold, public servant: papers rel to Yugoslavia c1940–79 (MSS. Eng. c.2683–90, 2695, 2713)

Edmund Brisco Ford (1901–88), geneticist: papers

Nikolaas Tinbergen (1907–88), ethologist: papers

Sir Hugh Carleton Greene (1910–87), director-general of the BBC: papers

George Alfred George-Brown, Baron George-Brown (1914–85), politician (addnl): papers

Sybil, Lady Colefax: papers 20th cent

REGENT'S PARK COLLEGE,
ANGUS LIBRARY, PUSEY STREET,
OXFORD OX1 2LB

Richard Hall, Baptist minister: notebooks containing hymns written by Benjamin Beddome 1774–95, misc letters to him 1846–1907

Saffron Walden General Baptist Trust: accounts and papers 1854–1921

Burgh and Monksthorpe Baptist Church: records 1692–1858

Potters Bar Baptist Church: church books 1802–94

Sandhurst Baptist Church: church book 1761–1851

North London Baptist Ministers Fraternal: minute book 1934–47

RHODES HOUSE LIBRARY,
SOUTH PARKS ROAD,
OXFORD OX1 3RG

David Bradshaw, educationalist in Ghana: papers rel to Achimota College and teacher training 1948–72

Reginald Leslie Cheverton: tour diaries and notebooks 1942–63, and photograph albums 1928–47, rel to his work with the Colonial Medical Service in Ghana and Nigeria

Sir Geoffrey Francis Taylor Colby, governor of Nyasaland: papers 1948–56

James Ecroyd, Quaker emigrant to Natal: letters to his family 1850–53

Harwicke Holderness, Southern Rhodesian lawyer and politician: papers rel to political history of Rhodesia 1945–58

Edward Ross Townsend, British South Africa Co and Southern Rhodesian administrator (addnl): corresp and papers incl letters from Earl Grey and Cecil Rhodes 1895–1906

THE MIDDLE EAST CENTRE,
ST ANTONY'S COLLEGE,
OXFORD OX2 6JF

Hassan Barnaba Dehqani-Tafti (b1920): papers as president-bishop of the Episcopal Church in Jerusalem and the Middle East

Sir Richard Augustus Vaux (1869–1946), colonial judge: memoirs of Egypt

PUBLIC RECORD OFFICE OF NORTHERN IRELAND

66 BALMORAL AVENUE,
BELFAST BT9 6NY

Montgomery family of Blessingbourne, co Tyrone: papers incl those of Captain Peter Montgomery c1880–1977

Montgomery family of co Down and Northumberland: papers rel to Elsdon 1597–1908

Workman family, shipbuilders and engineers, Belfast: legal papers 1901–25

GAM Gillespie: papers incl as Clogher Area Medical Officer for the Ulster Special Constabulary and the Ulster Home Guard 1939–46

Frederick Temple Hamilton-Temple-Blackwood, 1st Marquess of Dufferin and Ava (addnl): private in-letters incl from his parents 1835–95

Harford Montgomery Hyde (1907–89), author and barrister: papers

Christopher J Napier, solicitor: papers rel to the public enquiry into the events of Sunday, 30 January 1972 in Londonderry

East Downshire Steam Ship Co Ltd, steam ship owners, later East Downshire Ltd, coal merchants, Dundrum: records 1847–1980

Belfast and District Trades Union Council minutes 1925–34

Irish Transport and General Workers Union Dockers Committee, Belfast branch: records incl papers of Paddy Devlin, author and trade unionist c1930–78

Ulster Farmers Union (addnl): records 1918–88

Ulster Head Masters Association records 1917–86

National Council for Carers and their Elderly Dependants, Belfast branch (addnl): records 1970–87

Northern Ireland Citizens Advice Bureau, Portadown branch (addnl): records 1972–89

Northern Ireland Health and Social Services Training Council: minutes and papers 1969–89

Northern Ireland Training Authority: minutes and papers 1964–90

Staff Commission for Education and Library Boards: minutes and papers incl those of staff councils administered by the commission 1973–90

Social Democratic and Labour Party (addnl): records 1972–86

Aghadowey and Agivey Relief Committee, co Londonderry: records 1847–1957

Londonderry Port and Harbour Commissioners (addnl): records 1869–1987

Register of freeholders, co Armagh 1804–30

READING UNIVERSITY

UNIVERSITY LIBRARY,
WHITEKNIGHTS, READING RG6 2AE

Nancy Astor, Viscountess Astor (addnl): letters received 1930–58 (MS 3748)

George Allen, publisher: letters received 1883–1906 (MS 3745)

Gerald Pegnall: letters received as secretary of Leeds University English Society 1972–74 (MS 3743)

George Bell & Sons Ltd, publishers, London (addnl): corresp, financial and legal papers 1838–1943 (MS 3741)

Working Party on Library and Book Trade Relations (LIBTRAD): minutes and conference papers 1963–81 (MS 3746)

RELIGIOUS SOCIETY OF FRIENDS

FRIENDS HOUSE, EUSTON ROAD,
LONDON NW1 2BJ

Friends Ambulance Unit (addnl): papers rel to the China convoy 1939–47 (TEMP MSS 876)

ROYAL BOTANIC GARDENS

LIBRARY AND ARCHIVES,
KEW, RICHMOND, SURREY TW9 3AB

Leslie Hall (1900–91), viscose chemist: papers rel to the economic uses of plants and plant chemistry (Acc 91–14)

Gerald Walter Erskine Loder, 1st Baron Wakehurst (1861–1936), tree and shrub collector: papers (Acc 91–06)

ROYAL NAVAL MUSEUM

HM NAVAL BASE,
PORTSMOUTH PO1 3LR

William Foy: diary as captains cook during the commission of HMS *Prince Regent* 1848–50 (355/91)

Rear-Admiral Sir Ernest John Spooner: midshipmans journal 1906–07 (181/91)

Captain B Knightley Boase RN: letters (43) written during World War I (89/91)

Commander CS Sheppard: midshipmans journals (2) 1925–28 (101/91)

Chief Petty Officer C Simpkin: memoir of service as engine room artificer during World War II (1/91)

ST ANDREWS UNIVERSITY

UNIVERSITY LIBRARY,
NORTH STREET, ST ANDREWS,
FIFE KY16 9TR

Balfour family of Fernie: papers 17th–20th cent (ms 38262-71)

Cheape family of Strathtyrum: family and estate papers 19th–20th cent (ms Dep 76)

Gilmour family, baronets, of Lundin and Montrave: family papers 19th–20th cent (ms Dep 73)

Margaret Gatty (1807–73), childrens writer and naturalist: albums (3) (ms 38224)

Alexander Macduff (1792–1842), of Bonhard: commonplace book (ms 38277)

William Carmichael M'Intosh (1838–1931), zoologist: papers rel to the Royal Commission on Trawling 1884 (ms 38225)

Andrew Lang (1844–1912), folklorist and poet: letters and papers (ms 38233–61)

James Wilkie Nisbet (1903–74), professor of political economy: lecture notes (ms 38272–73)

SCIENCE MUSEUM LIBRARY

LONDON SW7 5NH

Ernest Cranstoun Given (1870–1961), director of airship production, Admiralty: papers (Acc 1991–317)

Ted Hamel: reminiscences rel to the testing of *Bluebird* and the death of Donald Campbell 1966–67 (Acc 1991–264)

Bramah & Robinson, machinists and engineers, London: engineering drawings (17 vols) c1804–59 (Acc 1991–349)

Glass Houghton & Castlefield Collieries Ltd: minute book 1946–56 (Acc 1991–326)

London Warming & Ventilating Co, stove mfrs: ledger 1856–68 (Acc 1991–338)

SCOTTISH CATHOLIC ARCHIVES

COLUMBA HOUSE, 16 DRUMMOND
PLACE, EDINBURGH EH3 6PL

Blairs College (addnl): records incl reports and corresp 1900–86 (CB)

SCOTTISH RECORD OFFICE

HM GENERAL REGISTER HOUSE,
EDINBURGH EH1 3YY

Carmichael family of Skirling, Peeblesshire (addnl): estate papers 1877–1961 (GD89)

Dick-Cunyngham family, baronets, of Prestonfield, Midlothian (addnl): papers 1627–1917, incl corresp rel to Sir Robert Keith Dick-Cunyngham's art collecting in Italy 1844–47 (GD1/1123)

Douglas family of Strathendry, Fife: family and estate papers 1477–1883, incl corresp rel to the Darien Scheme 1698–99 (GD446)

Erskine family of Cardross, Stirlingshire (addnl): legal and estate papers 1532–1865 (GD15)

Oswald family of Cavens, Kirkcudbrightshire and Auchincruive, Ayrshire (addnl): legal and estate papers 1536–1868 (GD213)

James Wilson, zoologist, and Sir James Alexander Russell, lord provost of Edinburgh: corresp and misc papers 1748–1927 (GD1/1121)

Alexander Cowan & Sons Ltd, paper mfrs, Penicuik (addnl): deeds and financial records 1709–1937 (GD311)

St Marys, Banff (addnl): kirk session records 1644–1965

SHEFFIELD UNIVERSITY

UNIVERSITY LIBRARY, WESTERN BANK, SHEFFIELD S10 2TN

Charlotte Joanne Erickson (b1923), historian: research papers rel to the steel industry

John Douglas Eshelby (1916–81), materials scientist: corresp and papers

SOCIETY OF ANTIQUARIES OF LONDON

BURLINGTON HOUSE, PICCADILLY, LONDON W1V 0HS

Bryan Faussett (1720–76), antiquary: *Collecta Parochiala*, notes on monuments and epitaphs of Kentish churches and churchyards; Kentish pedigrees including copies of Philipot's Visitation of Kent 1619–21 and part of Bysshe's Visitation 1663 (MSS 920–21)

SOUTHAMPTON UNIVERSITY

UNIVERSITY LIBRARY, HIGHFIELD, SOUTHAMPTON SO9 5NH

Arthur Wellesley, 1st Duke of Wellington (1769–1852), (addnl): corresp and papers (c400 items), incl political corresp 1827–52; corresp with his private secretary Lt-Colonel John Gurwood and his confidential servant Christopher Collins; and Collins personal papers (MS69)

Norman J Crisp, television and film writer: papers incl scripts, short stories and novels, and papers of the Writers Guild of Great Britain c1956–86 (MS199)

Jewish Care: records of predecessor bodies incl the Board of Guardians for the relief of the Jewish Poor; the Jewish Association for the Protection of Girls, Women and Children; and the Jewish Blind Society 1757–1989 (MS173)

STRATHCLYDE UNIVERSITY

UNIVERSITY ARCHIVES, GLASGOW G1 1XQ

Sir George Lionel Pepler (1882–1959), town planner (addnl): papers (T–PEP)

SUSSEX UNIVERSITY

MANUSCRIPTS SECTION, UNIVERSITY LIBRARY, BRIGHTON BN1 9QL

Frances Birrell: corresp and papers rel to work in France for the War Victims Relief Committee of the Society of Friends 1915–20

TATE GALLERY ARCHIVE

MILLBANK, LONDON SW1P 4RG

Wells Wintemute Coates, architect: corresp rel to history of Unit One artists group 1933–35 (9120)

CGH Dicker, painter: letters to his aunts rel to life as a student at the Slade School of Fine Art 1925–29 (9119)

Thomas Wade Earp, writer: corresp and MSS 1937–55 (9124)

Peter Fuller, art critic and editor of *Modern Painting*: corresp and MSS c1960–90 (9123)

Henri Gaudier-Brzeska, sculptor: corresp with Kitty Smith 1907–15 (9115)

Max Gordon, architect: corresp and papers rel to his art collection 1975–90 (9127)

Sir Geoffrey Alan Jellicoe, architect: corresp with Ben Nicholson rel to collaboration on a landscape design project 1960–73 (919)

Eileen Mayo, painter, illustrator and writer: records incl corresp, drawings and proof wood-engravings 1923–51 (916)

Charlotte Murray, collector: corresp with and rel to Stanley Spencer 1945–70 (9118)

Lady 'Peter' Norton, collector and founder member of the Institute of Contemporary Arts: records incl corresp c1950–72 (9113)

Sir William Newenham Montague Orpen, painter: letters to Sir William McComish rel to his portrait 1917–28 (9126)

Dame Ethel Sands, painter: corresp and family papers 1896–1952 (9125)

Felicity Samuel Gallery, London: corresp and business papers 1971–85 (914)

VICTORIA AND ALBERT MUSEUM

ARCHIVE OF ART AND DESIGN, 23 BLYTHE ROAD, LONDON W14 0QF

Crafts Council records 1971–86 (AAD 4–1991)

Crown Suppliers, producers and suppliers of furniture for the public service: drawings and papers c1930–90 (AAD 1–1991)

Madame Crystal Ltd, ladies glove mfrs, and A Tugendhat, yarn importer, London: records 1928–90 (AAD 6–1991)

Nelson and Edith Dawson, silversmiths and decorative artists (addnl): designs, papers and corresp c1904–39 (AAD 9–1991)

Harold Felber, fashion designer: season books for the House of Brenner 1961–65, and sketches c1930–80 (AAD 13–1991)

Moira Forsyth (1905–91), stained glass artist: designs, papers and corresp (AAD 10–1991)

Sigrid Hunt (later Roesen), fashion illustrator and editor: drawings and papers 1938–71 (AAD 2–1991)

Isobel Designs Ltd, court dress mfrs, London: sketches and documentary material c1920–65 (AD 12–1991)

Sir James Morton and Morton Sundour Fabrics Ltd (addnl): papers and corresp 1887–1937 (AAD 3–1991)

Gaby Schreiber (d1991), consultant designer for industry: papers, diaries and designs (AAD 11–1991)

WARWICK UNIVERSITY

MODERN RECORDS CENTRE, UNIVERSITY OF WARWICK LIBRARY, COVENTRY CV4 7AL

David Clive Jenkins (b1926), trade union leader (addnl): office files and autobiographical papers (MSS.79/CJ)

Peter Nicholas, trade union convenor: papers rel to shop stewards organisation in The Rover Co Ltd and British Leyland UK Ltd c1950–79 (MSS.309)

Trades Union Congress (addnl): files pre-1960 (MSS.292)

Amalgamated Engineering Union (addnl): Southall district council records incl minutes, membership records and files rel to local employers 20th cent (MSS.259)

Manufacturing, Science and Finance Union (addnl): records of the Association of Scientific, Technical and Managerial Staffs and other constituent unions 20th cent (MSS.79)

National Union of Teachers records 1873–1967 (MSS.179)

Clothing Export Council minutes 1965–83 (MSS.222/CE)

WELLCOME INSTITUTE FOR THE HISTORY OF MEDICINE

183 EUSTON ROAD, LONDON NW1 2BN

Department of Western MSS

Johannitius (810–77): fragment of 14th cent text of his *Isagoge* (ms.6811)

Sir Thomas Barlow, Bt (1845–1945), physician (addnl): corresp and papers (Acc 348412)

William Thomas Brande, chemist: letters received 1825–66 (ms.6827)

Robert Dunn, surgeon: letters received 1846–76 (ms.6819)

Lyon Falkener, physician and surgeon: papers 1861–1939 (mss.6802-9)

Robert Whytt (1714–66), physician: papers (Acc 348843)

Thomas Burden & Co, chemists, London: prescription books 1863–1911 (mss.6217-19)

Medico-Botanical Society of London: letters and papers 1812–52 (ms.6824)

Edinburgh Royal Infirmary: casebook of cases treated by Robert Graham and James Home 1827–28 (ms.6053)

Contemporary Medical Archives Centre

Sir Christopher Howard Andrewes, virologist: papers incl entomological and ornithological diaries and research notebooks rel to influenza and the common cold 1911–33

Edward John Mostyn Bowlby (1907–90), child psychiatrist: corresp and papers (PP/BOW)

Siegmund Heinrich Foulkes (1898–1976), psychoanalyst and founder of the Group-Analytic Society: papers (PP/SRF)

Sir William Arbuthnot Lane (1856–1943), surgeon: papers and autobiographical notes (GC/127)

Stephen Lock: corresp as editor of the *British Medical Journal* 1975–91 (PP/LOC)

Sir Robert Reynolds Macintosh (1897–1989), professor of anaesthetics: diaries and corresp (PP/MAC)

Sir Edward Eric Pochin, physician and pioneer in radiation protection: corresp and papers c1960–79 (PP/POC)

Marthe Louise Vogt, pharmacologist: laboratory note books and corresp c1941–89 (PP/VOG)

Clare Winnicott, psychoanalyst: papers incl draft publications c1950–69

Action on Smoking and Health (ASH): records c1971–91 (SA/ASH)

The Physiological Society records 1876–c1991 (transferred from Churchill College, Cambridge) (SA/PHY)

Queen's Nursing Institute records c1890–1991 (SA/QNI)

Strangeways Research Laboratory, Cambridge (addnl): papers rel to early history of the laboratory (f1912), Dame Honor Bridget Fell (1900–86), and the Strangeways family (SA/SRL)

WESTMINSTER ABBEY MUNIMENT ROOM AND LIBRARY

LONDON SW1P 3PAY

Westminster Dean and Chapter: estate records (c9,000 items), mainly deeds but incl court rolls, rentals, surveys, terriers, particulars and valuations c1585–1940

WINDSOR: ST GEORGE'S CHAPEL

THE AERARY, ST GEORGE'S CHAPEL, DEAN'S CLOISTER, WINDSOR CASTLE SL4 1NJ

Derek Ian Tennent Eastman (1919–90), canon of Windsor: research notes rel to cult of John Schorn (d1314), rector of North Marston, Buckinghamshire

YORK MINSTER ARCHIVES

YORK MINSTER LIBRARY
DEAN'S PARK, YORK YO1 2JD

Tobie Matthew, archbishop of York: sermons preached before Henry Hastings, 3rd Earl of Huntingdon, lord president of the Council of the North 1591 (MS Add 582)

YORK UNIVERSITY

BORTHWICK INSTITUTE OF HISTORICAL RESEARCH, ST ANTHONY'S HALL, YORK YO1 2PW

Tuke family, Quaker philanthropists, of York (addnl): corresp, commonplace books and albums c1830–70 (Acc 25/91)

WH Brook, architectural historian: notebooks and photographs, mostly of York buildings c1890-1917 (Acc 50/91)

Association of University Teachers, York University branch: records c1965–90 (Acc 28–29/91)

Local Repositories: England

AVON

BRISTOL RECORD OFFICE, B-BOND WAREHOUSE, SMEATON ROAD, BRISTOL BS1 6XN

Samuel Gilbert Bateman, of Kingswood: family corresp and cycling tour notebooks 1893–1949 (Acc 40364)

Joseph McPherson, teacher and British agent in Egypt: letters and papers c1900–45 (Acc 40382)

Bristol Stock Exchange: minutes, corresp and financial records 19th–20th cent (Acc 40361)

Spears Bros & Clark Ltd, provision merchants: deeds, minutes and stock transfer records 1896–1960 (Acc 40363)

Trapnell & Forbes, solicitors, Bristol: deeds 19th–20th cent (Acc 40344)

BEDFORDSHIRE

BEDFORDSHIRE RECORD OFFICE, COUNTY HALL, BEDFORD MK42 9AP

Shuttleworth family of Old Warden (addnl): account books 20th cent (SL)

Wootton Pillinge manor court roll c1485–1547 (Z 710)

FM Gardner (1908–80), president of the Library Association and librarian at Luton: corresp and papers (Acc 6981)

Frederick T Cox, printer and stationer, Potton (addnl): records c1960–80 (X 704)

JR Eve & Son, land agents, surveyors and valuers, Bedford: records 1890–1930 (Z 720)

Alfred Ginn, forage contractor and corn merchant, Potton: records 1895–1909 (Z 723)

Greene King & Sons plc, brewers (addnl): records of predecessor companies incl Newland & Nash Ltd and Wells & Winch Ltd (GK)

National Union of Teachers, Bedfordshire division (addnl): records 1953–81 (X 394)

Bedford Constituency Labour Party (addnl): records 20th cent (X 494)

Bedfordshire Scout Association records 1914–91 (X 619)

Royal British Legion, Leighton Buzzard branch: minute book 1952–56 (Z 508/5)

Bedford Television Society records 1949–52 (Z 709)

Eversholt Friendly Society records 1876–1930 (X 783)

Sandy Fur and Feather Society records 1910–63 (X 779)

Eversholt Parochial Charities records 1734–1976 (X 782)

BERKSHIRE

BERKSHIRE RECORD OFFICE,
SHIRE HALL, SHINFIELD PARK,
READING RG2 9XD

Mecey family of Thatcham: household account book 1878–96 (D/EZ 81/2)

Richard Townsend, mayor and town clerk of Newbury: account books 1802–19 (D/EZ 81/1)

Charles Midwinter & Son, corn and seed merchants, Newbury: records 1865–94 (D/EX 1109)

Wantage Rural Deanery: chapter minutes 1855–91 (D/RDWT)

Abingdon United Reformed Church records 1712–1978 (D/N)

Silchester Methodist Circuit: records 1844–1983 (D/N) (transferred from Hampshire Record Office)

BUCKINGHAMSHIRE

BUCKINGHAMSHIRE RECORD OFFICE,
COUNTY HALL,
AYLESBURY HP20 1UA

Jenney family, of Drayton Beauchamp: deeds and estate papers 1648–1923 (Acc AR 56/91)

Stanhope family, Earls of Chesterfield: Buckinghamshire estate surveys and tenancy register c1760–1810 (D/X 1099)

Waller family, of Hall Barn, Beaconsfield: deeds and estate papers 1632–1831 (D/X 1122)

John Hicks Graves, clergyman: corresp and papers some rel to the Oxford Movement 1840–77 (D/X 1167)

Alliance Assurance Co Ltd, Aylesbury office: policy registers 1875–1953 (Acc AR 18/91)

Collingwood family, printers, Wooburn: deeds and papers rel to Lower Glory paper mills 1665–1865 (Acc AR 38/91)

Lucas & Powell, solicitors, Newport Pagnell: out-letter book rel to the proposed Wolverton and Bedford branch railway 1845–46 (D/X 1097)

National Union of Teachers, Aylesbury and district association: minutes 1906–57 (Acc AR 123/91)

Charndon Association Football Club minutes 1931–35 (D/X 1109)

Oddfellows, Loyal Band of Hope Lodge, Haddenham: subscription book 1896–1916 (PR 87)

Hambleden parish registers 1566–1969 (PR 89)

CAMBRIDGESHIRE

COUNTY RECORD OFFICE,
SHIRE HALL, CAMBRIDGE CB3 0AP

Cutting family of Manea Fen and
Canada: letters and papers incl those of
Samuel Crump of Pittsford, Michigan
1839–88 (R91/46)

Over inclosure commissioners minutes
1837–44 (R91/57)

Cambridgeshire Growers Ltd, wholesale
fruit merchants, Longstanton: minutes
1950–76 (R91/56)

Hudson's Cambridge & Pampisford
Breweries Ltd: deeds 1713–1973,
business records 1888–1949
(R91/26–27)

Spicers Ltd, manufacturing stationers,
Sawston: records incl deeds, and papers
rel to Bridewell precinct 1611–1991
(R91/78)

Eastern Counties Liberal Federation:
records 1920–88 (R91/32)

Cambridgeshire and Isle of Ely General
Benefit Society: records 1842–1985
(R91/17, 31)

Cambridge Preservation Society records
1928–75 (R91/8)

COUNTY RECORD OFFICE,
GRAMMAR SCHOOL WALK,
HUNTINGDON PE18 6LF

John Gilbert, local historian, Wansford
(addnl): collected papers 1869–1983
(4051)

Godmanchester view of frankpledge
1499 (4056)

Cooper's Hospital, Elton: records
1760–1963 (4079)

Deacon's Charity, Peterborough:
accounts 1776–1877 (4026)

Peterborough United Charities records
1572–1967 (3901)

Perry Baptist Chapel records 1842–1982
(4047)

CHESHIRE

CHESHIRE RECORD OFFICE,
DUKE STREET, CHESTER CH1 1RL

Egerton family, Barons Egerton of
Tatton (addnl): corresp and papers
1728–83 (DET 4674)

Foden, Cooper and Davies family of
Sandbach and Elworth: papers
19th–20th cent (D 4519)

Cholmondeley Hall estate map 1781
(DCH 4605)

Eaton Hall: plans and elevations by
Samuel Cockerell and Lewis Wyatt
1813–28 (D 4637)

Imperial Chemical Industries plc
(addnl): records c1789–20th cent
(DIC 4623)

William and John Moore,
wheelwrights, Dutton: account books,
notebooks and corresp 1843–1910
(D 4606)

Amalgamated Society of Woodworkers,
Congleton branch: registers, accounts
and papers c1865–1973 (LOU 9/4609)

Chester and North Wales Incorporated
Law Society minutes 1881–1936
(D 4614)

Congleton Air Training Corps accounts
1941–56 (LOX 20/4611)

Crewe Music and Arts Society: records
incl minutes and accounts 1946–91
(D 4627)

CHESTER CITY RECORD OFFICE,
TOWN HALL, CHESTER CH1 2HJ

Coopers Company records 1422–1991
(G7)

William Edward Lindop & Son,
drapers: records incl accounts, staff
records and corresp 1884–1974 (CR641)

Postmens Federation Mutual Benefit
Society, Chester branch: records
1898–1930 (CR633)

Chester Archaeological Society (addnl): records 1869–1985 (CR75)

Upton Village Hall Committee minutes 1926–58 (CR651)

CLEVELAND

CLEVELAND ARCHIVES SECTION, EXCHANGE HOUSE, 6 MARTON ROAD, MIDDLESBROUGH TS1 1DB

Middlesbrough Long Distance Swimming Club minutes 1965–70 (Acc 2335)

Middlesbrough Rotary Club: records incl minutes 1921–81 (Acc 2355)

South Stockton Mechanics Institute: minutes and accounts 1862–91 (Acc 2394)

Middlesbrough Local Medical Committee minutes 1954–77 (Acc 2383)

CORNWALL

CORNWALL RECORD OFFICE, COUNTY HALL, TRURO TR1 3AY

Arundell family, Barons Arundell of Wardour: Lanherne deeds, estate and manor records, household papers and corresp 12th–19th cent (AR)

Penrose family of Penryn: papers 1744–1842 (BRA 2509)

Sir Goldsworthy Gurney (1793–1875), inventor: papers (X 843)

John Sansom, architect, Liskeard: plans of churches and public buildings 1840–20th cent (X 847)

British and Foreign Bible Society, Lostwithiel action group (addnl): records 1889–1986 (X 848)

Captain Hutchens Charity, Paul: records 1741–1991 (P172)

Cornwall Council of Churches: minutes 1970–91 (X 835)

Falmouth and Penryn Congregational churches: records 1780–1969 (X 850)

CUMBRIA

CUMBRIA RECORD OFFICE, THE CASTLE, CARLISLE CA3 8UR

Hudleston family of Hutton John (addnl): corresp and diaries 1844–1914 (D/Hud)

David Imrie, gamekeeper, Braithwaite: diaries, poems and drawings 1927–86 (DX/1288)

British Gypsum Ltd, plasterboard mfrs, Penrith: minutes and photographs 1951–77 (DB/121)

Carlisle & North Western Counties Savings Bank (addnl): minutes, accounts and ledgers 1818–1979 (DB44/10)

West Cumberland By-Products Co Ltd, chemical mfrs, Flimby: ledgers and registers 1910–80 (DB/122)

National Farmers Union: regional, county and branch minutes 1918–83 (DSo/135)

Cumbrians for Peace: minutes and corresp 1979–87 (DSo/133)

CUMBRIA RECORD OFFICE, COUNTY OFFICES, KENDAL LA9 4RQ

Bigland family of Bigland Hall: family and estate papers 1803–1964 (WD/Bgld)

Waistell family of Waitby: deeds and papers 1593–1824 (WDX/1026)

Kendal corn rents: assessment books, collectors books and papers 1834–1985 (WDX/1013, WDX/1043)

Maulds Meaburn manor rental 1587 (WD/CAT)

John Ruskin, author and artist: corresp with H Fletcher and HD Rawnsley 1875–85 (WDX/1039)

Alice Smith, Grange-over-Sands: papers rel to vernacular architecture, particularly cruck barns of Cumbria and North Lancashire 20th cent (WDX/1015)

Alfred Wainwright, writer: drawings and papers rel to guides to the Lakeland Fells c1950–89 (WD/AW)

Braithwaite & Co Ltd, woollen mfrs, Kendal (addnl): records 1888–1966 (WD/HCW)

Isaac Braithwaite & Son (Drysalters) Ltd, Kendal (addnl): account books 1893–1929 (WD/HCW)

Isaac Braithwaite & Son Engineers Ltd, Kendal (addnl): corresp 1930–56 (WD/HCW)

Kentmere Ltd, cardboard box mfrs, Staveley: deeds and papers rel to mills 1784–1903 (WDB/106)

Tom Sayer and Albert Shaw, blacksmiths, Brough Sowerby: ledgers 1907–59 (WDB/107)

Staveley Cinema Co Ltd: minutes and accounts 1947–56 (WDB/108)

National Union of Teachers, Westmorland County Teachers Association: minutes 1903–74 (WDSo/96)

Westmorland Liberal Association: minutes, ledgers and accounts 1900–71 (WDSo/174)

United Nations Association of Great Britain and Northern Ireland, South Westmorland district: minutes 1923–49 (WDSo/175)

Appleby Choral Union: minutes and accounts 1899–1965 (WDSo/172)

Hutton Roof Navvies Reading Room: corresp and accounts 1890–1945 (WDSo/171)

Kendal Guild of Service/Citizens Advice Bureau (addnl): minutes, corresp and accounts 1939–72 (WDSo/2)

Kirkby Lonsdale and District Gardening Association (addnl): records 1885–1991 (WDSo/120)

South Cumbria Girl Guides Association (addnl): records 1915–84 (WDSo/42)

Westmorland Agricultural Society (addnl): minutes 1972–87 (WDSo/78)

Kirkby Stephen United Charities (addnl): minutes 1912–76 (WDEC/17)

Sedbergh United Charities and Widows Hospital: deeds, minutes, accounts and corresp 1879–1979 (WDEC/18)

CUMBRIA RECORD OFFICE,
140 DUKE STREET,
BARROW-IN-FURNESS LA14 1XW

National Union of Teachers, Barrow and District Teachers Association: minutes 1881–1923 (BDSo/56)

Grange-over-Sands and District Volunteer Fire Brigade: records incl corresp c1905–24 (BDSo/54)

Ulverston Womens Institute Market records 1970–91 (BDSo/55)

North Lonsdale bridgemasters book 1777 (BDX/246)

DERBYSHIRE

DERBYSHIRE RECORD OFFICE,
EDUCATION DEPARTMENT,
COUNTY OFFICES, MATLOCK DE4 3AG

John Biggs (1909–88), wood engraver and typographer: corresp and papers (D3562)

John Smedley Ltd, hosiery mfrs, Lea Mills, nr Matlock: records 1854–1954 (D3546)

Chesterfield Transport records 20th cent (D3493)

DEVON

DEVON RECORD OFFICE,
CASTLE STREET, EXETER EX4 3PQ

Bere family of Huntsham and
Morebath: records incl deeds and rentals
1587–c1935 (D 4770)

Hole family of Parke, Bovey Tracey
(addnl): accounts and papers 17th
cent–1960 (D 312 add 8)

Luxmoore family of Okehampton
(addnl): household accounts and papers
1815–1951 (D 4739 and adds 1–3)

Seymour family, Dukes of Somerset
(addnl): deeds, corresp and drawings
1583–1916 (D 3799 add 2)

Wills family of Lustleigh: deeds and
papers 1630–1913 (D 4855)

Luscombe estate and Dawlish manor:
records incl court books 1722–1926
(D 4765)

Stockland manor: rentals, accounts and
papers 1721–1936 (D 4858)

Commercial Union Assurance Co Ltd
(addnl): policy registers of the West of
England Fire and Life Assurance Co
1813–72 (D 4293 adds 2–3)

George Langdon Fulford, solicitor,
Okehampton and North Tawton:
clients papers 1799–1906 (D 4817)

Paish & Co (1937) Ltd, musical
instrument dealers, Torquay: stock
books and customer register 1897–1963
(D 4827)

Whiteways Cyder Co Ltd, Exeter:
records incl deeds, accounts, corresp and
minutes 1825–1987 (D 4801)

Exeter Conservative Association minutes
1979–85 (D 4850)

Devon Federation of Young Farmers
Clubs (addnl): records incl accounts
1937–84 (D 2696 add 53)

Exeter Round Table (addnl): minutes
and corresp 1938–91 (D 4443 add)

Devon and Cornwall Architectural
Society, Exeter branch: minutes and
corresp 1916–67 (D 4851)

East Devon Hunt (addnl): minutes,
accounts and papers 1900–81 (D 3270
add 4)

Lympstone Cricket Club: corresp and
scoring books 1950–61 (D 4822)

Royal Devon Yeomanry Trust and
Royal Devon Yeomanry Old Comrades
Association: corresp and papers 1963–89
(D 4823)

Company of Weavers, Fullers and
Shearmen of Exeter (addnl): drawings
of Tuckers Hall 1789–1944 (D 4339
add)

Torquay Central Library: MS collection
incl deeds, charity papers, ships log
books and protests 1756–1940 (D 4826)

NORTH DEVON RECORD OFFICE,
TULY STREET, BARNSTAPLE EX32 7EJ

Maurice Prince (d1990), cinema
proprietor: diary and papers (B200)

John Hannaford & Son, auctioneers,
valuers and land agents, Chulmleigh:
records 18th–20th cent (B229)

North Devon Clay Co Ltd (addnl):
records c1920–65 (B188)

Torrington Industrial Co-operative
Society Ltd: accounts 1901–59 (B213)

Barnstaple Amateur Operatic Society:
minutes 1938–84 (B227)

North Devon Film Society (addnl):
records 1949–85 (B193)

Appledore United Reformed Church
records 17th–20th cent (B151)

WEST DEVON AREA RECORD OFFICE,
UNIT 3, CLARE PLACE, COXSIDE,
PLYMOUTH PL4 0JW

William Truman Harris, shipowner, of
Plymouth: records incl accounts
1828–38 (1326)

Plymouth Youth Orchestra minutes
1951–73 (1334)

Records of Ford Street Almshouses,
Tavistock 1922–83, and Maynard's
Charity, Tavistock 1862–83 (1324)

Plymouth Free School: account book
and minutes 1832–56 (1333)

Oyster Fishery, Cattewater, Plymouth:
leases of fishing rights 1764–1870
(1322)

*Transferred from Lyme Regis (Philpot)
Museum (D/LRM)*

Edmund Prideaux of Forde Abbey:
commonplace book c1710

Conservative Party, Charmouth branch:
minutes 1924–52, incl womens
association minutes 1930–36

Royal Society for the Prevention of
Cruelty to Animals, Lyme Regis and
Charmouth branch: minutes 1892–1981

DORSET

DORSET RECORD OFFICE,
BRIDPORT ROAD,
DORCHESTER DT1 1RP

Paget family, Marquesses of Anglesey
(addnl): Stalbridge estate papers
1640–1854 (D/ANG)

Milton Abbas manor court roll with
customs 1754 (D.1168)

Puddletown manor perambulation 1890
(D/BOP)

Capital & Counties Electric Theatres
Ltd, cinema owners, Bournemouth:
minutes and register of members
1919–69 (D.1157)

Panton & Co, brewers, maltsters, wine
and spirit merchants, Wareham and
Swanage: records incl deeds and
accounts 1774–1897 (D.1170)

W & J Tod Ltd, motor boat builders,
Weymouth: accounts 1942–74
(D/TOD)

White and Bennett families, brewers,
Wareham: deeds and papers 1750–1885
(D.1167A)

St Margaret's and Stones Charity,
Wimborne Minster (addnl): records incl
accounts and rentals 1896–1980
(D/SMS)

Sherborne School: records incl
foundation charter, deeds, statutes,
estate papers, minutes, orders, letter
books and school rolls 1550–1984
(S.235)

DURHAM

COUNTY RECORD OFFICE, COUNTY
HALL, DURHAM DH1 5UL

Bourne family of Cotherstone: deeds
and papers 1696–1955 (D/X 938)

Richard Atkinson, clergyman, and
Elizabeth his wife: diaries and corresp
1818–60 (D/X 946)

Thomas Rudd, vicar of St Oswald,
Durham: notebook 1711–28 (D/X 952)

Durham County Association of Trades
Councils: records 1974–90 (D/X 953)

Darlington Queens Nursing Association
minutes 1939–63 (D/X 955)

National British Womens Total
Abstinence Union, Barnard Castle
branch: minutes 1923–57 (D/X 954)

Darlington Town Mission: minutes incl
Darlington Charity Organisation Society
1852–1972 (D/X 944)

Parish records of Brignall 1588–1989
(EP/Bri); and Rokeby 1589–1988
(EP/Rok) (partly transferred from
North Yorkshire County Record
Office)

ESSEX

ESSEX RECORD OFFICE, COUNTY
HALL, CHELMSFORD CM1 1LX

Bennett family, Collier Row: papers
17th cent–c1964 (D/DU 1591)

Capel Cure family of Blake Hall
(addnl): papers incl sketch books
c18th–20th cent (D/DCc, D/DU 1579)

Lawrence family, Brentwood: cash book
and ledgers c1890–1987 (D/DU 1597)

Majendie family of Hedingham Castle:
family and estate papers 1339–1968
(D/DMh)

Elizabeth Ogborne: papers rel to the
publication of *The History of Essex*
1813–81 (D/DU 1578)

Philip Arthur Wright, historian of
agricultural technology: notes and
papers 1920–85 (D/DU 1589)

Basildon Development Corporation
records 1949–87 (A/TB)

JR Eve & Son, land agents, surveyors
and valuers, Hitchin: papers and
workbooks rel to rate valuation in
Romford Union 1895–1928 (D/F 170)

Edward May, baker and confectioner,
Purleigh: ledgers, bills and corresp
1924–82 (D/F 160)

Brentwood Trades Council: minutes
and papers c1980–86 (D/Z 159)

British Soviet Friendship Society, South-
East Essex branch: minutes and papers
1978–82 (D/DU 1590)

Abbess and White Roding
Conservation Society: papers 1968–84
(D/Z 231)

Chelmsford Clerical Book Club:
minutes, accounts and corresp
1844–1984 (D/Z 217)

Forest and Harlow Educational
Fellowship: papers 1935–72 (D/Z 167)

Ugley Village Hall: accounts, minutes
and papers c1924–80 (D/Z 228)

ESSEX RECORD OFFICE, COLCHESTER
AND NORTH-EAST ESSEX BRANCH,
STANWELL HOUSE, STANWELL
STREET, COLCHESTER CO2 7DL

Dunnett family of Little Bromley:
estate records 1776–1963 (Acc C468)

Kerridge and Cutting families of
Bradfield and Wix: business records
1884–1903 (D/F 99)

Rentals of the manors of Dedham Hall,
and Overhall and Netherhall 1762–83
(D/P 26)

E Marriage & Son Ltd, flour millers,
corn, hay and seed merchants,
Colchester: 1884–1952 (D/DJ)

Alfred Water Norfolk, carriers,
Brightlingsea: financial records 1907–25
(D/F 165)

ESSEX RECORD OFFICE, SOUTHEND
BRANCH, CENTRAL LIBRARY,
VICTORIA AVENUE,
SOUTHEND-ON-SEA SS2 6EX

Byford Brothers Ltd, builders
merchants, Southend-on-Sea: records
c1900–85 (D/F 172)

GLOUCESTERSHIRE

GLOUCESTERSHIRE RECORD OFFICE,
CLARENCE ROW, ALVIN STREET,
GLOUCESTER GL1 3DW

Blathwayt family of Dyrham Park
(addnl): family papers (D2659)

Avening manor court rolls and jury
presentments 1799–1831 (D6389)

Francis Wickens & Hill, solicitors,
Stow-on-the-Wold (addnl): deeds and
clients papers 17th–20th cent (D4084)

John Jeffries & Son Ltd, seed
merchants, Cirencester: records 1819–85
(D6464)

Little & Hutton, solicitors, Stroud
(addnl): clients papers incl records of
Strachan & Co Ltd, woollen mfrs
1865–1948; Sherbourne Lodge of
Freemasons 1822–1965; and Ceylon
estate papers of John Phipps of
Pitchcombe 1920–62 (D1815)

HH Martyn & Co Ltd, architectural
metal workers, Cheltenham (addnl):
records incl foundry managers papers
c1900–66 (D5922)

Cheltenham and District Trades
Council (addnl): records incl minutes
and secretarys files 1967–86 (D3614)

Transport and General Workers Union:
records of the South West region and
Gloucester district, and of predecessor
bodies incl the National Union of
Agricultural and Allied Workers,
Gloucester district 20th cent (D6375)

Gloucester Citizens Advice Bureau
(addnl): day books c1981–87 (D3911)

Gloucestershire Federation of Womens
Institutes: committee minutes and
records of defunct institutes c1918–89
(D6381)

National Association of Prison Visitors,
Gloucester branch: minutes 1925–88
(D6504)

Ashleworth Cricket Club: minutes and
accounts 1935–52 (P20a)

Blockley Antiquarian Society: MS
collection rel to Blockley 9th–20th cent
(D3471)

Gloucester Port customs and excise
book 1736–66 (D6471)

Winchcombe Town Trustees (addnl):
records incl papers rel to George
Townsend Charity Trustees 16th–20th
cent (D1675)

HAMPSHIRE

HAMPSHIRE RECORD OFFICE,
20 SOUTHGATE STREET,
WINCHESTER SO23 9EF

Acland family, baronets, of Columb
John, Devon: letters and papers incl
those of Lady Harriet Acland 19th–20th
cent (103M91)

Bonham-Carter family, of Adhurst St
Mary (addnl): records incl deeds and
accounts 1492–1744 (70M88)

Herbert family, Earls of Carnarvon:
corresp and papers 18th–19th cent
(75M91)

William James Harris, 6th Earl of
Malmesbury (addnl): papers c1970–89
(68M91)

Barker Son & Isherwood, solicitors,
Andover (addnl): records incl clients
papers and manorial records 15th–20th
cent (46M84)

James Duke & Son Ltd, millers,
Bishops Waltham: deeds and business
records 1708–1980 (4M91, 17M91)

Michelmersh Brick & Tile Co Ltd:
records 1949–70 (12M91)

HN Thornton & Sons, tailors,
Winchester: records 1910–63 (113M91)

Central Electricity Generating Board,
Marchwood Engineering Laboratories:
records c1960–90 (48M91)

National Union of Teachers, Hampshire
division: records 1961–87 (112M91)

Old Contemptibles Association,
Basingstoke branch: records 20th cent
(52M91)

Ringwood Unitarian Church records
1695–1896 (41M91)

King Alfreds College of Education,
Winchester: records 19th–20th cent
(47M91)

St Johns Winchester Charity: records
incl deeds, corresp, minutes and
accounts 16th–20th cent (34M91)

Itchen Navigation (addnl): deeds and papers 1712-1957 (15M91)

Hook House, Titchfield: building account book 1785-91 (39M91)

Naval Ordnance Museum, Gosport: MS collection incl maps, plans, technical drawings, Admiralty fleet orders, and Ordnance Board corresp 17th-20th cent (109M91)

PORTSMOUTH CITY RECORDS OFFICE, 3 MUSEUM ROAD, PORTSMOUTH PO1 2LE

HMS *Dryad*: log from England to Africa 1830-32; in back of vol accounts of J Croad Ltd, builders, Portsea 1840-45 (PCRO 1703A/1)

SOUTHAMPTON CITY RECORDS OFFICE, CIVIC CENTRE, SOUTHAMPTON SO9 4XR

Francis Barton, corn merchant: ledgers 1908-21 (D/Z 889)

Panton & Co, brewers, Wareham: records rel to tied premises in Southampton 1884-96 (D/Z 894)

Paris Smith & Randall, solicitors (addnl): records incl clients papers 1720-1958 (D/PSR)

Southampton Chamber of Commerce minutes 1851-86; Southern Fruit and Potato Merchants Association minutes 1942-64 (D/COM)

Institution of Production Engineers, Southampton section (addnl): minutes 1972-91 (D/Z 733)

Trojans Rugby Union Football Club: minutes 1874-1902 (D/Z 877)

HEREFORD AND WORCESTER

HEREFORD AND WORCESTER RECORD OFFICE, COUNTY HALL, SPETCHLEY ROAD, WORCESTER WR5 2NP

Vernon family, baronets, of Hanbury (addnl): records 18th-19th cent (BA 10794)

Great Malvern manor court rolls 1729-1909, and Holt manor court rolls 1729-58 (BA 10935)

Tardebigge manor records incl court rolls c1594-1931 (BA 10343)

Talbot & Talbot, solicitors, Kidderminster: records incl clients papers 19th-20th cent (BA 10894)

Evesham Borough (addnl): minute and order books 17th cent (BA 10822)

HEREFORD AND WORCESTER RECORD OFFICE, THE OLD BARRACKS, HAROLD STREET, HEREFORD HR1 2QX

Hereford family of Sufton: deeds and estate papers 1514-1879

Pudleston Court estate: deeds 18th-20th cent

Westhide estate: deeds 19th cent

William Elrington, teacher: letters from St Petersburg 1795-1860

Hereford Race Course: accounts and corresp 1862-75

Pulling & Co Ltd, wine merchants, Hereford: accounts and papers 19th-20th cent

Kilvert Society: records incl corresp with William Plomer 20th cent

Jarvis Charity, Staunton-on-Wye: deeds, accounts and minutes 1749-1990

HERTFORDSHIRE

HERTFORDSHIRE RECORD OFFICE,
COUNTY HALL, HERTFORD SG13 8DE

GM Hopkins, Royal Flying Corps:
World War I logbook (Acc 2671)

Leslie G Bland, electrical engineer,
Hertford: contract books 1922–42
(Acc 2609)

British Aerospace plc: technical records
of predecessor companies incl De
Havilland Aircraft Co Ltd, Hatfield
c1940–89 (Acc 2653)

Christy family, Westbury Farm,
Ashwell: farm accounts 1795–1871
(Acc 2661)

John Cooper & Sons, ironmongers,
Hertford: records 1898–1958 (Acc 2654)

JW French & Co Ltd, millers, Ware:
records 1923–51 (Acc 2603)

Gravesons Ltd, drapers, Hertford:
records incl cash books 1874–1940
(Acc 2642)

James Lewis, chemist, Ware:
prescription books 1840–1900
(Acc 2601)

Simpson's Brewery Ltd, Baldock
(addnl): records 1826–1964 (Acc 2623)

Hertfordshire League of Hard of
Hearing: records 1944–91 (Acc 2644)

Trustees of Ware Charity Estates
(addnl): records 15th–19th cent
(Acc 2626)

HUMBERSIDE

HUMBERSIDE COUNTY ARCHIVE
OFFICE, COUNTY HALL,
BEVERLEY HU17 9BA

Wilson family: papers rel to Hull,
Beverley, Newcastle upon Tyne and
military service in the West Indies 18th
cent; Griffith and Boynton families of
Burton Agnes estate papers and
manorial records 14th–18th cent;
Southwell Minster account roll 1437–38
(DDWn)

Richard Cooper, founder, ironmonger
and grocer, Goole: accounts and papers
c1862–1900 (Acc 2461)

Hull Savings Bank, Withernsea branch:
records 1928–80 (DDTS)

Powell & Young, solicitors,
Pocklington (addnl): clients papers incl
records of the Grant, Watford and
Bingham families, Pocklington, and
Welshpool, Montgomeryshire
1824–1922 (DDPY)

SOUTH HUMBERSIDE AREA ARCHIVE
OFFICE, TOWN HALL SQUARE,
GRIMSBY DN31 1HX

Mary Dannatt of Barrow Haven: diary
1858–65 (Acc 400/11)

Grimsby Institution of Engineers and
Shipbuilders (addnl): records 1909–69
(Acc 340)

Grimsby, Cleethorpes and District Free
Church Federal Council records
1944–91 (Acc 472)

Killingholme Baptist Church records
1686–1956 (T 54)

Matthew Humberstone School,
Cleethorpes: records 1821–1991
(Acc 166/722)

Grimsby parliamentary poll book 1831
(Acc 470)

KENT

CENTRE FOR KENTISH STUDIES,
COUNTY HALL, MAIDSTONE ME14 1XQ

Bromley family of Groombridge: papers
19th–20th cent (U3059)

John Ulick Knatchbull (b1924), 7th
Baron Brabourne, film and television
producer (addnl): business files (U951
addl)

John Mace, surgeon: diary 1825–42
(U3039)

Medway Navigation Co (addnl): deeds,
plans and agreements 1809–1937 (U3045)

Typographical Association, Kent area: minutes and papers 1897–1972 (U3022)

National Union of Teachers, Maidstone district: minutes 1944–54 (Ch102)

Canterbury and Rochester Joint Diocesan Council for Social Responsibility (addnl): minutes 20th cent (Ch69 addl)

Educational Institute of Design, Craft and Technology, Kent branch: records 1912–72 (Ch98)

Beult Sunday School Union minutes 1961–75 (Ch53 addl)

Hothfield Education Foundation minutes 1910–90 (Ch101)

Rochester Theological College minutes 1959–70 (DRa addl)

MEDWAY AREA ARCHIVES OFFICE, CIVIC CENTRE, STROOD, ROCHESTER ME2 4AW

Joseph Collis Ltd, ironmongers, Strood: records 1751–1981 (DE 113, 122)

Kidwell & Son, surveyors, auctioneers and estate agents, Rochester: building plans for Medway Towns c1900–55 (DE 121)

National Union of Teachers, Chatham and Rochester association: minute books 1874–1962 (DE 155)

Valuation lists for Chatham, Gillingham, Rochester and Strood 1935–75 (DE 117)

Transferred from Centre for Kentish Studies, Maidstone

Bligh family, Earls of Darnley: family and Cobham Hall estate papers 1537–c1940 (U 565)

Records of parishes in Cobham, Dartford and Gravesend rural deaneries 14th–20th cent (P)

SHEPWAY BRANCH ARCHIVES OFFICE, CENTRAL LIBRARY, GRACE HILL, FOLKESTONE CT20 1HD

King & Chasemore, estate agents and valuers, Lyminge: records c1920–60 (F1991/4)

THANET BRANCH ARCHIVES OFFICE, RAMSGATE LIBRARY, GUILDFORD LAWN, RAMSGATE CT11 9AI

Benefield & Cornford, estate agents and valuers, Birchington: records c1920–85 (R/U87)

LANCASHIRE

LANCASHIRE RECORD OFFICE, BOW LANE, PRESTON PR1 2RE

Preston Borough: records incl charters and guild rolls 1199–1972 (CNP)

Addison family of Preston: papers 19th cent (DDPm)

Stanley family, Earls of Derby (addnl): estate papers 19th–20th cent (DDK)

Woodhouse family of Stalmine: papers 16th–20th cent (DDX 1908)

AE Gilfillan, town clerk of Barnsley: papers 1895–1937 (DDX 1903)

John Lingard, historian: letters 1821–37 (RCHy)

British Tufting Machines Ltd, Blackburn: records 1954–70 (DDX 1869)

Grane Manufacturing Co Ltd, cotton fabrics mfrs, Haslingden: records 1907–78 (DDX 1870)

Stephen Simpson Ltd, gold thread mfrs, Preston: financial records 19th–20th cent (DDX 1876)

C Whittaker & Co Ltd, brick-making machinery mfrs, Accrington (addnl): records 19th–20th cent (DDX 1866)

Winckley Club, Preston: records
c1844–1968 (DDX 1895)

Leicestershire Constabulary (addnl):
records incl predecessor bodies
c1838–1960 (DE 3831)

LEICESTERSHIRE

LEICESTERSHIRE RECORD OFFICE,
57 NEW WALK, LEICESTER LE1 7JB

Packe family of Prestwold (addnl):
papers c1850–1970 (DE 3969)

Manton manor court rolls 1767–1934
(DE 3821)

William Tom Hind, chemist, Leicester:
prescription books 1894–1951
(DE 3827)

J Pick & Sons Ltd, fancy hosiery mfrs,
Leicester: records 19th–20th cent
(DE 3859)

Stephen Taylor & Son, organ builders,
Leicester: accounts and papers
1872–1928 (DE 3814)

Wilkinson Hardware Stores (Leicester)
Ltd: records c1930–91 (DE 3808)

Wootton Brothers Ltd, iron and brass
founders and engineers, Coalville:
records 1894–1948 (DE 3843)

Leicestershire Trade Protection Society
(addnl): records incl those of the
Nottinghamshire and Derbyshire
Traders Association, and the Association
of Trade Protection Societies of the
United Kingdom 1850–1982 (DE 3848)

National Union of Teachers: records of
Leicestershire district branches 1921–85
(DE 3984)

National Union of Boot and Shoe
Operatives: Barwell and Earl Shilton
branch records c1889–1989 (DE 3989)

Leicester Young Mens Christian
Association (addnl): records 1885–1986
(DE 3901)

Leicester and Leicestershire
Photographic Society records 1883–1991
(DE 3868)

Leicester General Charities (addnl):
records 19th–20th cent (DE 3832)

LINCOLNSHIRE

LINCOLNSHIRE ARCHIVES,
ST RUMBOLD STREET,
LINCOLN LN2 5AB

Osburne family of North Kelsey: deeds
and papers 1550–1631 (Acc 91/83)

Haxey Hall Garth manor court books
1740–1916 (Acc 91/154)

George Tennyson d'Eyncourt of Bayons
Manor: journals 1839–57 (Acc 91/4)

Louth Savings Bank and Louth Penny
Bank: records c1850–20th cent
(Acc 91/93)

Nettleship & Lucas, estate agents and
auctioneers, Market Rasen: records
19th–20th cent (Accs 91/157, 91/160)

National Farmers Union of England and
Wales, Lincolnshire (incl South
Humberside) branch: records 1904–80
(Acc 91/113)

Lincoln Musical Society records 1934–80
(Acc 91/45)

Heightington Infant Welfare Clinic
records 1930–78 (Acc 91/59)

Horncastle Childrens Home records
1933–46 (Acc 91/111)

GREATER LONDON

GREATER LONDON RECORD OFFICE,
40 NORTHAMPTON ROAD,
LONDON EC1R 0HB

Basil Futvoye Marsden-Smedley, barrister
and public servant, and his wife Hester:
papers c1900–80 (Acc 2908)

Aerated Bread Co Ltd, bakers: minutes,
register of premises 1869–85 (Acc 2909)

Watney Mann Ltd, brewers (addnl):
minutes and photographs 1898–1973
(Acc 2979)

National Union of Teachers, London
County branch: minutes 1906–66
(Acc 2902)

Greater London Labour Party (addnl):
records incl corresp c1965–80
(Acc 2959)

Benevolent Society of St Patrick: reports
and accounts 1784–1970 (Acc 2895)

Sarah Rachel Titford's Charity: minutes
and accounts 1845–1990 (Acc 2896)

Food for the Jewish Poor: minutes and
financial records 1872–1980 (Acc 2942)

Jewish Bread, Meat and Coal Society:
minutes, reports and financial records
1797–1954 (Acc 2944)

Kashrus Commission: ledgers, salary
records and koshering registers 1961–82
(Acc 2980)

London and Middlesex Archaeological
Society: records incl minutes and
accounts c1855–1990 (Acc 2899)

Sutton Housing Trust: records incl
minutes, accounts and tenants registers
1896–1989 (Acc 2983)

United Hospitals Club of St Thomas
and Guys Hospitals: minutes and
photographs c1822–1930 (Acc 2989)

Victoria Boys and Girls Clubs: minutes,
reports and corresp c1901–89 (Acc 2996)

Federation of Synagogues: records incl
minutes and corresp 1898–1976
(Acc 2893)

New Road Synagogue, Whitechapel:
corresp and financial records 1924–74
(Acc 2943)

Western Synagogue: minutes, accounts,
corresp and membership records
1767–1981 (Acc 2911)

West London Synagogue of British
Jews: financial records 1840–1970
(Acc 2886)

Royal Northern Hospital, Holloway;
Mildmay Memorial Hospital and
Hornsey Central Hospital: minutes,
financial and patients records 1856–1969
(Acc 2934)

CORPORATION OF LONDON
RECORDS OFFICE, PO BOX 270,
GUILDHALL, LONDON EC2P 2EJ

Spitalfields Market (addnl): account
books and register of tenants 20th cent

Guildhall School of Music and Drama
(addnl): records incl accounts and papers
rel to Dorothea Crompton c1880–1970
(GMSD)

GUILDHALL LIBRARY,
ALDERMANBURY, LONDON EC2P 2EJ

Ashanti Goldfields Corporation Ltd
(addnl): letter books and photographs
c1940–69 (Mss 24658–75)

Butterworth & Co (Publishers) Ltd:
records 1818–1975 (Mss 24606–49)

Buzzacott, Lillywhite & Co, chartered
accountants: clients account books
c1920–50

Chinese Engineering & Mining Co Ltd:
records c1900–50

Harrisons & Crosfield Ltd, general
merchants: records c1840–1955

Hodder & Stoughton Ltd, publishers
(addnl): author files c1970–89

Frederick Huth & Co, merchant
bankers (addnl): letters (c90) from
merchants in Spain 1812–48

London & Provincial Law Assurance
Society records c1870–89
(Mss 24549–51)

London Provident Institution Savings
Bank: ledgers 19th–20th cent

John Motteux & Co, merchants: letters
(11) received from Mr Palsy at L'Orient
1772–75 (Ms 24552)

James Vickers Ltd, isinglass merchants:
records 1867–1912 (Mss 24588–605)

T Wiggin & Co, American merchants:
records 1858–74 (Mss 24708–11)

BARNET ARCHIVES AND LOCAL
STUDIES CENTRE, RAVENSFIELD
HOUSE, THE BURROUGHS, HENDON,
LONDON NW4 4BE

Finchley Manor allotment: records
1951–71

BEXLEY LIBRARIES AND MUSEUMS
DEPARTMENT, LOCAL STUDIES
CENTRE, HALL PLACE, BOURNE
ROAD, BEXLEY, KENT DA5 1PQ

John Wells Wilkinson, curate of
Belvedere: papers mainly rel to
education, politics, and trade unionism
in Erith c1890–1959 (PE/JWW)

National Union of Teachers: records of
Erith Teachers Association 1905–64,
and Bexley Teachers Association
1944–59 (CS/NUT/E, CS/NUT/B)

BRENT LOCAL STUDIES LIBRARY,
GRANGE MUSEUM OF COMMUNITY
HISTORY, NEASDEN LANE,
LONDON NW10 1QB

T Roberts & Co, builders and
decorators, Cricklewood: account books
1902-13 (Acc 34/1988)

Amalgamated Society of Woodworkers,
Willesden branch: attendance registers,
account and letter books c1920–57
(Acc 14/1988)

CROYDON LOCAL STUDIES LIBRARY,
BEATRICE AVENUE, NORBURY,
LONDON SW16 4UW

Gillett & Johnson Ltd, clock mfrs and
bell founders, Croydon: records incl bell
and tuning books 1877–1985 (AR1)

Mission of Hope, childrens home and
adoption agency, Croydon: case files
c1900–50 (AR11)

GREENWICH LOCAL HISTORY
LIBRARY, WOODLANDS, 90 MYCENAE
ROAD, LONDON SE3 7SE

Winifred Langton: unpublished
biography 1989, and family papers of
Donald Adolphus Brown, foreman at
Woolwich Arsenal during World War
I (6999)

Cook family of Bostall Farm,
Plumstead: family papers 1823–1925

Dr George Rice (1848–1935), medical
superintendent of Woolwich Union
workhouse: papers

Greenwich Hutments Tenants League:
minutes and notebooks 1935–38
(6541–2)

HACKNEY ARCHIVES DEPARTMENT,
ROSE LIPMAN LIBRARY, DE BEAUVOIR
ROAD, LONDON N1 5SQ

A Sindall & Co, textile trimmings
mfrs, Dalston (addnl): records
1868–1987 (D/B/SIN)

Elizabeth Fry Probation Hostel,
Islington: records incl predecessor bodies
1806–1964; and British Ladies Society
for Promoting the Reformation of
Female Prisoners: records 1821–91
(D/S 58)

Robinson's Retreat and Robinson's
Relief Fund: records incl minutes
1812–1991 (D/S 57)

Women's National Cancer Control
Campaign, Hackney and district branch:
minutes and accounts 1964–90 (D/S 54)

HAMMERSMITH AND FULHAM
ARCHIVES AND LOCAL HISTORY
COLLECTIONS, THE LILLA HUSET,
191 TALGARTH ROAD, LONDON W6 8BJ

Belsham & Sons Ltd, printers: records
1913–73 (DD/775)

7th Fulham (Christ Church) Scout
Group records 1910–69 (DD/786)

Hampshire House Trust (addnl): minutes 1921–51 (DD/792)

Haringey Womens Training and Education Centre: records rel to Haringey Womens Employment Project c1980–89

Thomas Bentham, vicar of Beddington and antiquarian: MS collection incl household and estate corresp and papers of the Carew family, baronets, of Beddington 1567–1627 (32)

George Rice, physician: personal papers c1870–1930 (39)

Frederick Cavendish-Pearson, architect, Sutton: records rel to Sutton Garden Suburb c1908–50 (Acc 107)

David Hayes Dance Band, Wallington: papers 1929–48 (26)

Norwood Conservative Association: minutes and financial records 1875–1984 (1991/25)

Lambeth charities: records incl rel to Hayle's Charity and Walcot Charity 17th–20th cent (IV/165)

Stockwell Green United Reformed Church: minutes and financial records c1799–1989 (1991/26)

Cambridge and Bethnal Green Boys Club records 1937–87 (TH/8458)

Frederica Emma Hunter, Lady Hunter: diaries 1840–46 (Acc 1621)

Chrisp family: papers rel to local politics incl Deptford Labour Party 1928–70

Carrington & Co, jewellers: estimate and deposit books 1904–28 (Acc 1626)

Lewisham Lions Pentathlon Club records 1967–90

William Soper & Son, enamellers and enamel painters: formula and account books c1848–1901 (Acc 1627)

East Ham Hall manor court record book 1829–1904

Christopher Wright, art historian: papers c1974–90 (Acc 1628)

GREATER MANCHESTER

BOLTON ARCHIVE SERVICE, CENTRAL
LIBRARY, CIVIC CENTRE, LE MANS
CRESCENT, BOLTON BL1 1SE

Fletcher family of Bolton: Haulgh, Darcy Lever and Little Lever deeds and papers, and Alkrington colliery records 1611–1863 (ZFL)

Osman Textiles Ltd, Bolton: records 1874–1974 (ZZ/561)

Ancient Noble Order of United Oddfellows, Bolton Unity: Grand Lodge records 1831–1959 (FO/2)

Gosnell's Charity, Bolton: minutes and accounts 1830–1968 (FCH/3)

Popplewell Scholarship Charity, Bolton: minutes and accounts 1928–72 (FCH/4)

ROCHDALE LIBRARIES,
LOCAL STUDIES DEPARTMENT,
AREA CENTRAL LIBRARY,
ESPLANADE, ROCHDALE OL16 1AQ

Entwisle family of Foxholes: deeds (59) 12th–16th cent

STOCKPORT ARCHIVE SERVICE,
CENTRAL LIBRARY, WELLINGTON
ROAD SOUTH, STOCKPORT SK1 3RS

Stockport District Waterworks Co (addnl): minutes 1865–99 (D1663)

Halle Club, Cheadle and Gatley branch records 1948–90 (D1675); and Stockport and district branch records 1947–82 (D1687)

Stockport County Anglers Association minutes 1893–1934 (D1677)

Stockport Ragged and Industrial School, Offerton (addnl): register of girls progress after discharge 1919–23 (D1659)

TAMESIDE ARCHIVE SERVICE, ASTLEY
CHEETHAM PUBLIC LIBRARY,
TRINITY STREET,
STALYBRIDGE SK15 2BN

Philanthropic Mutual Life Assurance Collecting Society, Hyde: records 1832–1991 (Acc 2340)

Ashton Business and Professional Women's Club minutes 1951–72 (Acc 2320)

Hyde Society records 1968–91 (Acc 2350)

WIGAN ARCHIVES SERVICE,
TOWN HALL, LEIGH WN7 2DY

Burrows family, Atherton: papers 1871–1900 (Acc 2696)

Edward Leigh of Lowton: account books 1806–23 (Acc 2712)

Coop & Co Ltd, clothing mfrs, Wigan: records 1862–20th cent (Acc 2708)

Alfred Goulding Ltd, haulage contractors, Wigan: records 20th cent (Acc 2702)

J & J Hayes Ltd, cotton spinners, Leigh (addnl): records 1881–1972 (Acc 2755)

Wright & Appleton, solicitors, Wigan (addnl): deeds and papers (Acc 2703)

Wigan Music Society records 1948–90 (Acc 2753)

MERSEYSIDE

MERSEYSIDE RECORD OFFICE,
CUNARD BUILDING (4th FLOOR),
PIER HEAD, LIVERPOOL L3 1EG

Bootle and Liverpool fire brigades: papers incl photographs c1880–1970 (388MFS)

Owen Owen plc, departmental stores: records 20th cent (4756)

Royal Court Theatre: ledgers and misc papers c1950–69 (4831)

Association of Jewish Ex-Servicemen and Women, Merseyside branch (addnl): minutes 1964–90 (4821)

Mossley Hill Constituency Labour Party: records incl corresp 1984–86 (4840)

Royal Society of Chemistry, Liverpool section: records 1935–83 (4814)

Liverpool Business and Professional Women's Club: records incl minutes 1940–90 (4806)

Liverpool Stock Exchange: records incl minutes 1836–20th cent (4828)

Merseyside Trade Union Community and Unemployed Resource Centre: Library Group minutes and papers 1984–91 (4839)

Liverpool Board of Shechita: minutes and financial records 1904–75 (4803)

Hughes family of Sherdley Hall (addnl): papers 13th–19th cent (SH)

Haydock Lodge Private Mental Hospital: case book, ledgers and journal 1863–1908 (HL)

Thomas Webster, barrister: reports and minutes of evidence rel to Birkenhead Dock bills 1848–53 (YPX/59)

Cammell Laird Shipbuilders Ltd, Birkenhead (addnl): records incl minutes, accounts, plans and specifications c1820–1989 (ZCL)

United Nations Association of Great Britain and Northern Ireland, Birkenhead branch: records incl minutes 1936–91 (YUN)

Wirral Water Board minutes 1963–73 (A/WW)

WEST MIDLANDS

Lloyd family, bankers: letters from Alan Lloyd in South Africa 1900–14 (MS 1612)

Kings Norton manor records 17th cent (MS 1670)

Paul Mackney, socialist and trade unionist (addnl): papers mainly rel to Birmingham Trades Council c1970–90 (MS 1591)

Beacon Insurance Co Ltd, Birmingham: minutes, claims registers and staff records 1885–1967 (MS 1605)

Birmingham Mint Ltd: corresp c1930–60 (MS 1623)

British Jewellery and Giftware Federation Ltd: minutes, accounts, corresp and publications incl records of predecessor bodies 1851–1987 (MS 1646)

West Midlands Arts: records incl minutes and application registers 1957–89 (MS 1620)

Banner Theatre of Actuality: records incl administrative files c1974–90 (MS 1611)

Grey Cock Folk Club, Birmingham: records incl corresp 1978–87 (MS 1642)

Cadbury Trusts (addnl): grant files c1980–90 (MS 1579)

Harborne Parish Lands Charity: deeds, minutes, accounts and registers 1581–1980 (MS 1673)

Sir Josiah Mason Orphanage and Almshouses, Erdington: estate papers, minutes, accounts and registers 1854–1978 (MS 1609)

Birmingham Blue Coat School, Harborne: deeds, minutes, accounts and pupil records 1722–1988 (MS 1622)

Cannon Street Baptist Church, Birmingham: minutes, registers, accounts and corresp 1778–1986 (BC 2)

COVENTRY CITY RECORD OFFICE, MANDELA HOUSE, BAYLEY LANE, COVENTRY CV1 5RG

Hewitt family, Viscounts Lifford: deeds, corresp and family papers, incl papers of James Hewitt, 1st Viscount Lifford 18th–20th cent (Acc 1484)

Alvis Ltd, vehicle and aero engine mfrs (addnl): records 1934–86 (Acc 1454)

PS Burden & Co Ltd, builders: minute book and financial records 1923–50 (Acc 1450)

Cornercroft Ltd, vehicle and aircraft component mfrs: records incl subsidiary companies 1927–86 (Acc 1468)

Alfred Herbert Ltd, machine tool mfrs (addnl): records 20th cent (Acc 1512)

Rotherham & Sons Ltd, precision engineers and watch makers: records 18th–20th cent (Acc 1467)

Cappers Company: records incl account and order books 15th–20th cent (Acc 1494)

Drapers Company (addnl): minute book 1887–1942 (Acc 1495)

38th Coventry, Warwick Road, Scout group records 1923–78 (Acc 1502)

Coventry Photographic Society: minutes, attendance books and competition records 1944–58 (Acc 1509)

Enterprise Club for Disabled People: historic record book 1938–88 (Acc 1476)

Longford Fire Brigade: minute book 1916–20 (Acc 1491)

Luftwaffe target map of north Coventry c1940 (Acc 1479)

SANDWELL DISTRICT LIBRARIES, LOCAL STUDIES CENTRE, SMETHWICK LIBRARY, HIGH STREET, SMETHWICK, WARLEY B66 1AB

AE Andrews & Sons, blacksmiths, West Bromwich: ledgers and papers 1898–1952 (BS/A)

Edwin Danks & Co (Oldbury) Ltd, boiler mfrs: records 1896–1976 (BS/ED)

West Bromwich Afro-Caribbean Resource Centre: minutes, reports and corresp c1980–89 (Q/AC)

Sandwell Arts Council: papers 1988–90 (Acc 9111)

Plans of abandoned non-coal mines 1842-87 (G/HS)

WALSALL ARCHIVES SERVICE, LOCAL HISTORY CENTRE, ESSEX STREET, WALSALL WS2 7AS

National United Order of Free Gardeners, Darlaston and Willenhall branch: records c1912–20 (Acc 666)

Philip Donnellan (*b*1924), film and
television producer: papers (Acc 843)

Anthony Twentyman (1906–88),
sculptor: papers rel to art and artists
incl Barbara Hepworth and John Piper
(Acc 841)

Stirk Benton & Co, solicitors,
Wolverhampton: deeds and clients
papers 18th–20th cent (Acc 857)

Royal Aeronautical Society,
Birmingham and Wolverhampton
branch: records *c*1940–49 (Acc 845)

Wolverhampton Film Society (addnl):
records 1946–84 (Acc 860–61)

Plans of abandoned non-coal mines,
Wolverhampton area (Acc 831)

NORFOLK

NORFOLK RECORD OFFICE, CENTRAL
LIBRARY, BETHEL STREET,
NORWICH NR2 1NJ

Betts family of Forncett and Tibenham:
deeds, accounts and papers 1766–1902

D'Oyly family, baronets, of
Shottisham: accounts and papers
1637–1728

Gaff family of Great Witchingham:
farming and personal records *c*1900–70

Gurney family of Sprowston Hall: deeds
and papers 1798–1904

Kemp family of Gissing and Bracon
Ash: estate papers *c*1616–1859

Nugent family, baronets, of West
Harling: manorial records and accounts
1625–1928

Benjamin and Isaac Brown, wine
merchants, Norwich: letter book
1789–93

William Case, notary public, King's
Lynn: register of ships protests
1788–1808

Eastern Counties Omnibus Co Ltd,
Norwich: minutes, financial and staff
records *c*1890–1969

Gurney & Co, textile mfrs and yarn
importers, Norwich: letter books,
ledgers, sale and insurance records
1761–1832

Francis Hornor & Son, land surveyors
and estate agents, Norwich: records incl
survey books and clients papers
16th–20th cent

Hotel de Paris, Cromer: daily accounts
1936–47

Isaac Lenny, land surveyor: specimen
map book 1791

D Pearce, general practitioner, Diss:
financial and practice records *c*1920–60

Norfolk & Norwich & East Anglian
Trustee Savings Bank: records of Great
Yarmouth branch 1818–1981, and
Norwich branch 1829–1935

Stannard, Taylor & Taxtor, textile mfrs
and exporters, Norwich: letter books,
financial, stock and production records
1751–72

Diss Citizens Advice Bureau: interview
books and case files 1981–90

Norfolk Agricultural Association
(addnl): records incl minutes 1848–99

Norfolk Federation of Womens
Institutes: records incl of constituent
institutes 1918–82

Great Yarmouth and Filby Unitarian
churches records *c*1740–1979

NORTHAMPTONSHIRE

NORTHAMPTONSHIRE RECORD
OFFICE, WOOTTON HALL PARK,
NORTHAMPTON NN4 9BQ

Ironstone Royalty Owners Association:
records incl corresp and minutes 1943–86

Northamptonshire County Cricket
Club: records incl accounts and scoring
books 1892–1982

Law and Hutcheson's Charity, Kingscliffe: records 1623–1979

NORTHUMBERLAND

NORTHUMBERLAND RECORD OFFICE, MELTON PARK, NORTH GOSFORTH, NEWCASTLE UPON TYNE NE3 5QX

Sir Thomas Grey of Heaton and Chillingham: description of his possessions in North Northumberland c1568–89 (NRO.4118)

NOTTINGHAMSHIRE

NOTTINGHAMSHIRE ARCHIVES OFFICE, COUNTY HOUSE, HIGH PAVEMENT, NOTTINGHAM NG1 1HR

Lascelles family of Elston Hall: military records c1640–90 (Acc 4251)

Cahn family, baronets, of Stanford Hall: deeds, financial records of Sir Julien Cahn 18th–20th cent (Acc 4248)

Angular Hole Drilling & Manufacturing Co Ltd, machine tool mfrs, Beeston: records 19th–20th cent (DD 1596)

Sisson & Parker Ltd, booksellers, Nottingham: records incl accounts 20th cent (DD 1666)

James Shipstone & Sons Ltd, brewers, Nottingham: production records 20th cent (Acc 4129)

Nottingham Co-operative and Labour Party Central Division: minutes 1928–37 (DDPP 13)

British Soviet Friendship Society, Nottingham branch (addnl): minutes and corresp c1978–90 (DDPP 11)

Royal Institution for the Blind (East Midlands): papers 20th cent (DD 1604)

Trent Valley Soroptimist Club (addnl): records incl attendance lists 20th cent (DD SO)

Nottingham Inner City Executive files c1980–89 (Acc 4094)

Nottingham and District Sports Club for the Disabled: records incl minutes c1960–89 (DD 1575)

Nottingham Jewish Congregation: balance sheets 1904–44 (NC/JW)

OXFORDSHIRE

OXFORDSHIRE ARCHIVES, COUNTY HALL, NEW ROAD, OXFORD OX1 1ND

Belson family, Henley: papers incl diaries 19th–20th cent (Acc 3302)

Slaugham manor, Sussex: court rolls 1667–1799; and Down Barnes manor, Middlesex: court rolls 1793–1802 (Acc 3326)

Early's of Witney plc, blanket mfrs: records 17th–20th cent (Acc 3253)

British Beekeepers Association, Oxfordshire branch: records 1949–86 (Acc 3344)

Oxford City Moral Welfare Association records 1921–76 (Acc 3226)

Oxford and District Private Fire Brigades Association records 1923–89 (Accs 3315, 3329)

Oxford Womens Centre records 1980–91 (Acc 3353)

Pyrton Charity records 1674–1902 (Acc 3235)

Witney Monthly Meeting of the Society of Friends: records incl deeds 1637–1796 (Acc 3292)

SHROPSHIRE

SHROPSHIRE RECORD OFFICE, SHIREHALL, ABBEY FOREGATE, SHREWSBURY SY2 6ND

Edwards family of Great Ness (addnl): family papers 19th cent (5358)

Morris family of The Hurst, Clun, and Pentre-Nant, Churchstoke (addnl): estate papers 17th–20th cent (5692)

John Flavel of Cleobury Mortimer:
diary 1791–97 (5665)

Henry Sherwood of Bridgnorth: diaries
rel to European travel and with the
army in the West Indies and India
1791–1815 (5624)

Hampton Loade ironworks: account
book 1819–36 (5686)

Sun Insurance Office Ltd, Shrewsbury
(addnl): records incl minutes 1886–1988
(4791)

SOMERSET

SOMERSET RECORD OFFICE, OBRIDGE
ROAD, TAUNTON TA2 7PU

Dickinson family of Kingweston and
Lanhydrock (addnl): corresp 19th cent
(DD/DN)

Napper or Napier family of Tintinhull:
papers 16th–19th cent (A/ADZ)

Trevelyan family, baronets, of
Nettlecombe (addnl): corresp and papers
16th–17th cent (DD/MCH)

General Richard Ford William Lambart,
7th Earl of Cavan: corresp aand papers
1804–13 (DD/BR/gnn)

Bennett & Co, land agents and
surveyors, Bruton: records incl letter
books and accounts 1818–1975
(DD/S/CM, DD/BT)

Clarke, Willmott & Clarke, solicitors,
Bridgwater: records incl clients papers
18th–20th cent (DD/CWCbw)

Gribble, Booth & Taylor, estate agents
and valuers, Minehead and Williton:
records 1900–91 (DD/GBM,
DD/GBW)

George Pollard & Co Ltd, timber
merchants and contractors, Taunton:
records incl accounts 1852–1970
(A/ADR)

North Somerset Constituency Labour
Party: records incl minutes and accounts
1918–79 (A/AAW)

Taunton Amateur Operatic Society:
records incl minutes and accounts
1900–85 (A/ACO)

STAFFORDSHIRE

STAFFORDSHIRE RECORD OFFICE,
COUNTY BUILDINGS, EASTGATE
STREET, STAFFORD ST16 2LZ

Bridgeman family, Earls of Bradford
(addnl): papers of 6th Earl and
Countess 1949–82 (D1287)

Hopkins family of Anslow: deeds and
estate papers 17th–19th cent (D5081)

Meakin family of Darlaston Hall: family
and estate papers 1835–1974 (D4998)

Watts-Russell family of Ilam (addnl):
deeds and estate papers 1709–1878
(D5046)

Sir Jeffry Wyatville, architect: plans for
alterations to Teddesley Hall 1818
(D5036)

Amalgamated Society of Woodworkers,
Smethwick branch: minutes 1876–1937
(D5051)

Staffordshire Drug and Health Project:
sample returns 1990 (D5027)

West Midlands Planning Authorities
Conference, Forum of County Councils
and Regional Forum: minutes and
subject files 1965–90 (D5045)

SUFFOLK

SUFFOLK RECORD OFFICE, IPSWICH
BRANCH, GATACRE ROAD,
IPSWICH IP1 2LQ

Manorial records of Ulveston 1318–61,
and Ulveston and Sackvilles 1541–1839
(HD 1480)

WS Cowell Ltd, printers, Ipswich:
records 1872–1970 (HC 439)

Edward S Singleton Ltd, funeral
directors, Ipswich: records 1872–1977
(HC 440)

Sun Insurance Office Ltd: Woodbridge agency ledgers 1877–1917 (HH 402)

National Union of Labour Organisers and Election Agents, East Anglia district: records incl minutes 1950–79 (GG 410)

Sudbury and Woodbridge Constituency Labour Party: minutes and branch records 1948–88 (GK 403)

Woodbridge Mutual Benefit Society minutes 1870–76 (HD 1496)

Gislingham United Charities records 1872–1974 (GB 428)

Needham Market Pest Houses Charity records 1812–1975 (GB 427)

SUFFOLK RECORD OFFICE, BURY ST EDMUNDS BRANCH, RAINGATE STREET, BURY ST EDMUNDS IP33 1RX

Cowlinge manor records 1792–1899 (HB 510)

Whepstead manor records 1726–1910 (HD 1740)

Evelyn Cockell of Eriswell: diaries 1904–33 (HD 1738)

Bury St Edmunds Sanitary Laundry: wages book 1928–38 (HC 532)

Greene & Greene, solicitors, Bury St Edmunds (addnl): records incl clients papers 1656–1936 (HB 500)

Amalgamated Society of Boilermakers, Shipwrights, Blacksmiths and Structural Workers, Bury St Edmunds branch: records incl minutes 1952–89 (GG 501)

Sudbury Divisional Labour Party: accounts 1932–36 (GK 502)

Bury St Edmunds Young Womens Christian Association: minutes 1941–51 (GC 536)

Bury St Edmunds Farmers Club records 1762–1955 (GC 534)

Risbridge Battalion of Volunteer Infantry: order book 1805–08 (HD 1741)

SUFFOLK RECORD OFFICE, LOWESTOFT BRANCH, CENTRAL LIBRARY, CLAPHAM ROAD, LOWESTOFT NR32 1DR

Fowler family of Gunton (addnl): estate accounts 1886–1900 (Acc 557)

Lt-General Sir Robert Rich, 5th Bt: notebook rel to inheritance dispute 1771–83 (Acc 541)

WE Wigg & Son, agricultural engineers, Barnby: customers accounts 1898–1915 (Acc 495)

London and North Eastern Railway: linesmans log books 1937–62 (Acc 519)

Lowestoft harbour (addnl): arrivals and sailings registers 1963–75 (Acc 507)

Beccles Society: minutes, corresp and papers 1966–89 (Acc 506)

Lord Kitchener Memorial Holiday Home, Lowestoft: minutes, registers and accounts 1919–87 (Acc 527)

SURREY

SURREY RECORD OFFICE, COUNTY HALL, PENRHYN ROAD, KINGSTON UPON THAMES KT1 2DN

Kilburn Priory: rental of lands held by the prioress in Leatherhead 1446 (3923)

Allfarthings manor map c1587–1649 (3991)

Barrow Green estate (addnl): deeds for Bletchingley, Surrey and Westerham and Edenbridge, Kent 1220–1626 (3920)

Unwin Brothers Ltd, printers, Woking (addnl): records 1876–1930 (3949)

National Union of Teachers: Surrey County Teachers Association records incl Epsom and Sutton, Carshalton and district, and St Helier local associations 1903–82 (3994)

Mole Valley Conservative Association records 1885–1983 (3960)

Wimbledon Young Mens Christian Association: records incl minutes 1901–87 (3952)

Merton and Morden Historical Society: records incl minutes 1951–65 (3913)

Rutlish School Debating Society minutes 1946–50 (3946)

Chertsey School for Handicrafts (addnl): minute book 1885–92 (3901)

St Mary, Bletchingley parish records c1538–1989 (3925)

SURREY RECORD OFFICE,
GUILDFORD MUNIMENT ROOM,
CASTLE ARCH, GUILDFORD GU1 3SX

Ind Coope & Co Ltd, brewers: deeds rel to licensed houses in South-West Surrey 1709–1930 (5020)

Newark Mill, Ripley: account book 1745–58 (5032)

Surrey Association of Trades Councils records 1974–91 (5017)

The Otherwise Club and Barn Theatre, Shere: records 1932–39 (5022)

Wey Arun Trust, Surrey section: corresp and papers 1970–84 (5036)

Guildford Meeting House of the Society of Friends: deeds and papers 1557–1964 (5021)

EAST SUSSEX

EAST SUSSEX RECORD OFFICE, THE
MALTINGS, CASTLE PRECINCTS,
LEWES BN7 1YT

Egerton family of Mountfield Court, and Brassey family of Normanhurst: family and estate papers 1864–1930 (A5634)

Micklethwait and Peckham families of Iridge: deeds and estate papers incl maps 1557–1892 (A5778)

Springett family of Hawkhurst, Kent and Salehurst: deeds and family papers 1625–1916 (A5639)

Thomas family of Ratton Park, Willingdon, and D'Oyly family of Buxted: papers 1711–1920 (A5648)

Hartfield Pashley manor court book 1626–1873 (A5716)

Rotherfield Rectory manor court book 1715–98 (A5770)

Ebenezer Johnston, minister of Westgate Unitarian Chapel: account book 1744–53 (A5697)

Norman Norris, museum curator and antiquarian, Brighton: personal and family papers 1867–1983 (A5709)

Philip Oxenden Papillon MP: diaries 1849–70 (A5709)

Pickard family, agents to the Glynde Estate Co: family and business records 1761–1955 (A5767)

The Southdown Building Society, Lewes: records of predecessors incl Lewes Co-operative Benefit Building Society and Eastbourne Mutual Building Society 1830–1979 (A5641, A5670, A5696)

The Grace Eyre Foundation, Hove: minutes 1940–84 (A5814)

Brookside Hounds, Ouse Valley: journals 1820–32 (A5709)

WEST SUSSEX

WEST SUSSEX RECORD OFFICE,
COUNTY HALL, CHICHESTER PO19 1RN

Dennett and Martin families of Henfield: family and estate papers 18th–19th cent (Acc 8607)

Bepton, Cocking, Linchmere, Shulbrede, Lurgashall, River, St John in Midhurst, Selham and Verdley manors: minutes 1825–1925 (Add MSS 42252–67)

Lancing manor court book 1762–1910 (Add MS 42996)

North Lancing and Monks South Lancing and Lyons manor: court books 1804-1924 (Add MS 42997-8)

Nyetimber manor accounts 1435-37 (Acc 8756)

EM Venables, geologist, of Bognor: scientific and personal papers (Acc 8588)

West Sussex Gazette & South of England Advertiser: records 1855-1947 (Add MSS 42876-42940)

West Sussex Permanent Benefit Building Society: records incl Littleton & District Building Society and Steyning & Littlehampton Building Society 1869-1970 (Acc 8814)

Milland Valley Horticultural Society: minutes 1906-64 (Acc 8774)

West Sussex College of Nursing and Midwifery records 1946-79 (Acc 8655)

United Nations Association of Great Britain and Northern Ireland, Chichester branch: records 1948-88 (Acc 8690)

Rural deanery records for Eastbourne c1870-1910 (Acc 8575), Pevensey 1840-60 (Acc 8576) and Storrington 1914-70 (Acc 8742)

TYNE AND WEAR

TYNE AND WEAR ARCHIVES SERVICE,
BLANDFORD HOUSE,
BLANDFORD SQUARE,
NEWCASTLE UPON TYNE NE1 4JA

Percy family, Dukes of Northumberland: Tynemouth agents corresp 1831-69 (Acc 2561)

CR Atkinson, accountant: papers incl records of ER Newbigin Ltd, shipping agents, Newcastle 20th cent; and Newcastle Dispensary minutes 1929-76 (Acc 2633)

William Ettrick, clergyman, of High Barnes, Sunderland (addnl): diaries, corresp and papers c1790-1860 (Acc 2539)

Maurice A Fraser (1906-90): papers rel to rugby in the North of England (Acc 2625)

Ralph Milbanke Hudson MP: constituency corresp c1920-30 (Acc 2557)

Brigham & Cowan Ltd, ship repairers, South Shields: financial and share records 1884-1903 (DX103)

William Cleland & Co Ltd, shipbuilders, Wallsend: register of members 1872-91 (Acc 2534)

County Hotel & Wine Co Ltd, wine merchants, Carlisle (addnl): records 1864-1985 (Acc 2550)

Crowley, Millington & Co, ironfounders, Swalwell and Winlaton: layouts of works 1718 (Acc 2644)

James D Johnson Ltd, coal merchants, Sunderland: financial records 1894-1960 (DX68)

WL Large & Sons Ltd, printers, Newcastle: financial records 1966-82 (Acc 2525)

Newcastle upon Tyne Savings Bank, Cullercoats branch: ledgers and abstracts 1931-75 (D/TSB2)

Raine & Co Ltd, iron and steel mfrs, Swalwell: minutes and financial records 1882-1972 (Acc 2529)

Sunderland Savings Bank (addnl): records incl minutes 1824-1969 (Acc 2523)

Sunderland & South Shields Water Co (addnl): minutes, financial, share and operational records 1834-1960 (Acc 2586)

Wearside Building Society: records incl minutes and ledgers 1930-70 (Acc 2580)

North-East Brewers Federation: records incl associated organisations 1875-1987 (Acc 2641)

Boys Brigade, North of England division: minutes 1922-77 (S/BB1); Newcastle battalion council minutes and statistics 1895-1982 (S/BB2-5)

British Ship Research Association: records incl Parsons and Marine Engineering Turbine Research and Development Association (PAMETRADA) c1949–67 (Acc 2570)

Educational Development Association, Sunderland branch: school camp logbooks 1928–89 (E/Su2)

Educational Institute of Design, Craft and Technology, Northumberland Tyne and Wear branch: records incl minutes c1928–90 (Acc 2522)

Modern Language Association, North East branch: records incl minutes and corresp 1939–89 (Acc 2560)

Workers Educational Association, Northern district: records incl minutes 1910–80 (Acc 2564)

Felling Allotments and House Garden Association: minutes and corresp 1976–89 (Acc 2573)

Poor Children's Holiday Association: records incl minutes, letter books and registers 1889–1972 (CH3)

National Garden Festival 90 (Gateshead) Ltd: records 1988–91 (Acc 2548)

Newcastle Maternity Survey 1960–69 and World Health Organisation Survey on women delivered at Princess Mary Hospital, Newcastle 1980 (Acc 2610)

North Shields crew lists and agreements c1863–1913 (transferred from Northumberland Record Office) (Acc 2599)

WARWICKSHIRE

WARWICKSHIRE COUNTY RECORD OFFICE, PRIORY PARK, CAPE ROAD, WARWICK CV34 4JS

Lowe family of Ettington, Quakers: corresp 1803–49

Ludford-Astley family of Ansley Park and Priest family of Fillongley and Birmingham: deeds, legal papers and corresp 1548–1812

Montagu-Douglas-Scott family, Dukes of Buccleuch (addnl): Boughton deeds and estate papers 1726–1934

Sanders family of Taff Farm, Astley: estate and personal papers 1868–1967

Octavia Pigott (née Cholmeley): diaries 1861–77

Thomas S Vernon: diaries recording visits to North Wales and life in Leamington 1797–1812

FT Woodfield of Alcester: MS collection incl records of Alcester Old Boys Football Club c1923–49, and Alcester Church Lads Brigade 1911, 1937–39

Hawkes/Cave-Browne-Cave, diocesan architects: files and plans rel to Warwickshire churches 1960–90

Society of Archivists, West Midlands region: records incl minutes c1950–84

Leamington and Warwickshire Soroptimists minutes 1968–79

Brinklow Pig Club: minutes and accounts c1885–1968

Swan Hotel Sick and Dividend Club, Kineton: subscription lists and accounts 1932–37

Warwick Boat Club (addnl): minutes 1868–96

Warwick charities: records incl those of Oken's and Griffin's charities 1799–1975

Arlidge's Charity, Kenilworth: records incl deeds and accounts 1608–1962

Leamington College of Art: headmasters report book 1930–48

Warwick Borough court leet proceedings 1939-90

Warwick Common herdsman's books 1853–1943

SHAKESPEARE BIRTHPLACE TRUST
RECORDS OFFICE, THE SHAKESPEARE
CENTRE, HENLEY STREET,
STRATFORD-UPON-AVON CV37 6QW

Beecham family of Clopton: estate
papers incl rel to Mursley,
Buckinghamshire 1632–1950 (DR 745)

Rice family of Alderminster and
Stratford-upon-Avon (addnl): family
papers incl corresp 17th–20th cent
(DR 724)

Archer & Coote, watch and clock
repairers, Stratford-upon-Avon: repair
registers 1950–88 (DR 725)

John Arthur Poyser, wheelwright,
Barkestone, Leicestershire: records
1919–58 (DR 717)

Shakespeare Head Press, Stratford-upon-
Avon: records incl letters to Arthur
Henry Bullen 1885–1931 (DR 719)

Shakespeare Club, Stratford-upon-Avon
(addnl): minutes 1944–91 (DR 734)

Stratford-upon-Avon Anti-Apartheid
Group records 1985–90 (DR 744)

ISLE OF WIGHT

ISLE OF WIGHT COUNTY RECORD
OFFICE, 26 HILLSIDE,
NEWPORT PO30 2EB

Bowerman family of Brook: rent book
1638–82, and rentals of the lands of
Thomas Worsley, a ward 1620–34
(91/39)

Appley Towers estate: accounts
1910–15 (91/45)

St Pauls Church Brotherhood, Barton:
records incl Junior Brotherhood
1910–40 (91/42)

Newport Charity Trustees: minute
books, letter books, account book and
registers 1837–1944 (91/23)

Wyndham Cottle Almshouses, Shalfleet:
accounts 1937–41 (91/33)

Isle of Wight Local Medical
Committee: corresp and papers 1936–78

WILTSHIRE

WILTSHIRE RECORD OFFICE, COUNTY
HALL, TROWBRIDGE BA14 8JG

Arundell family, Barons Arundell of
Wardour: deeds, manorial records and
estate papers rel to Wiltshire, Dorset
and Somerset; household and family
records incl papers of Sir Richard
Burton (1821–90), explorer and
diplomat; papers rel to the family's
Roman Catholic connections 15th–20th
cent (2667)

Talbot family of Lacock Abbey: deeds,
family and estate papers incl
Chippenham hundred court books
13th–19th cent (2664)

Arthur Barugh Thynne, vicar of Seend:
diaries 1869–1916 (2674)

Noah Butler, farmer and publican,
Worton: records incl ledgers and
accounts 1889–1911 (2679)

C Hoare & Co, bankers, London: deeds
and papers rel to Castle Combe and
West Ashton estates 16th–19th cent
(1494)

Martin and Stratford, estate agents,
Trowbridge: records incl clients papers
19th–20th cent (1039)

Mortimore & Son, coal merchants,
Chippenham: records incl ledgers and
accounts c1890–1980 (2668)

William G Salway, carpenter,
Chippenham: account book 1875–1933
(2645)

John Wallis Titt & Co Ltd, agricultural
and mechanical engineers, well borers,
sinkers and pump mfrs, Warminster:
records incl ledgers and plans of pumps
19th–20th cent (2574)

Unigate Foods Ltd, Trowbridge:
minutes, accounts and papers, incl
records of Wiltshire United Dairies Ltd
c1900–80 (1531)

West Midland Farmers Association Ltd,
agricultural merchants co-operative,
Melksham: minutes, ledgers and papers
20th cent (2591)

Wiltshire Association of Trades Councils: minutes and accounts 1965–90 (2648)

Incorporated Association of Organists: records incl minutes and accounts c1930–90 (1618)

Salisbury Radnor Lodge of Freemasons: minutes and papers 1922–80 (2677)

Trowbridge Town Association Football Club: records incl minutes 20th cent (2581)

West Wiltshire Golf Club: records incl minutes and accounts c1890–1980 (2643)

Wiltshire Lawn Tennis Association: records incl minutes 1948–87 (2670)

Wiltshire Scout Council: minutes, accounts and local troop records 20th cent (2636)

St John Association and Ambulance Brigade, Wiltshire: records incl minutes and accounts 20th cent (2611)

Dauntsey Earl Danbys Charity: minutes and accounts 19th–20th cent (1718)

Thomas Turnbull & Son, shipbuilders and owners, Whitby: plans and papers 1860–1906 (ZW)

Whitby shipbuilders and joiners accounts 1812–1924 (ZW)

British and Foreign Bible Society, Pickering branch: minutes, accounts and reports 1870–1917 (ZAX)

Independent Order of Oddfellows, Hovingham lodge: records incl minutes and membership register 1841–1948 (ZAX)

North Riding Territorial and Auxiliary Forces Association: records incl minutes 1908–67 (NG/TA)

Ripon charities (addnl): records 1672–1974 (DC/RIP)

York Conservative Club: minutes, accounts and membership records c1884–1989

NORTH YORKSHIRE

Hackness rent roll 1622–39 (TD 71)

Richmond manor records incl call rolls and presentments 1707–1831 (DC/RMB)

South Kilvington manor court book 1793–1805 (TD 69)

Thomas Daniels, Roman Catholic priest: account book 1750–75 (TD 72)

JH Barry & Co, shipowners, Whitby: records incl letter books, financial records and voyage books 1784–1853 (ZW)

Bedale Savings Bank: account books 1834–79 (ZAV)

SOUTH YORKSHIRE

AE Gilfillan, town clerk of Barnsley: papers c1900–88 (A/948, A/968)

Henry Elstone Ltd, tobacconists: records c1900–80 (A/965, A/973)

National Union of Teachers, Dearne Valley Teachers Association: minutes and accounts 1919–78 (A/1075)

Union of Shop, Distributive and Allied Workers, Barnsley British Co-operative Society Ltd branch: records 1931–87 (A/908)

Barnsley West Ward Labour Party and Barnsley South-West Ward Labour Party: minutes 1946–72 (A/985)

Barnsley Sunday School Union records
c1935–52 (A/1010)

Hickleton Main Death and Medical
Fund and Hickleton Main Miners
Welfare Scheme: records c1897–1973
(A/917)

Home coal delivery service records for
Darfield Main c1950–91, Dearne Valley
c1936–72 and Houghton Main 1927–90
(A/988, A/909, A/895)

DONCASTER ARCHIVES DEPARTMENT,
KING EDWARD ROAD, BALBY,
DONCASTER DN4 0NA

Warde-Norbury family of Hooton
Pagnell: family and estate papers
1826–1963 (DD.WN)

Doncaster Accident Rescue Team
records 1972–91 (DS61)

ROTHERHAM METROPOLITAN
BOROUGH ARCHIVES AND LOCAL
STUDIES SECTION, BRIAN O'MALLEY
CENTRAL LIBRARY, WALKER PLACE,
ROTHERHAM S65 1JH

JJ Habershon & Sons Ltd, steel strip
mfrs, Rotherham: plans of the Holmes
works 1822–60 (382/F)

National Union of Teachers,
Rotherham division: minutes and
corresp c1970–79 (374/G)

Feoffees of the Common Lands of
Rotherham: records incl deeds, minutes
and accounts 16th–20th cent (363/G)

SHEFFIELD ARCHIVES,
52 SHOREHAM STREET,
SHEFFIELD S1 4SP

World Student Games, Sheffield:
records 1991

Sir John Holbrook Osborn MP (addnl):
papers 1970–80

Guild of St George: corresp and papers
c1850–1970

National Union of Teachers,
Chapeltown and district association:
minutes 1931–76

Hallam Ward Labour Party minutes
1941–54

Ordnance Survey: minor control point
albums, South Yorkshire area c1940–50

Plans of abandoned non-coal mines,
Sheffield area c1930–80

WEST YORKSHIRE

WEST YORKSHIRE ARCHIVE SERVICE,
WAKEFIELD HEADQUARTERS,
REGISTRY OF DEEDS, NEWSTEAD
ROAD, WAKEFIELD WF1 2DE

Wentworth family, baronets, of
Bretton: papers 1647–1763 (C763)

Sir Horace Edwin Holmes MP: diaries
and notebooks 1915–59 (C795)

Alfred Leng, coachbuilder, Pontefract:
records 1889–1932 (C776)

Wakefield Power Station records
1953–91 (C796)

Medical Officers of Schools Association
records c1884–1980 (C724)

Pontefract Society of Friends Monthly
Meeting records 1628–1968 (C786)

WEST YORKSHIRE ARCHIVE SERVICE,
BRADFORD, 15 CANAL ROAD,
BRADFORD BD1 4AT

Samuel Cunliffe-Lister, 1st Baron
Masham (addnl): letters 1825–75
(24D91)

Jacob Moser, lord mayor of Bradford:
business and personal papers c1892–1922
(33D91)

Alhambra Theatre, Bradford (addnl):
records 1884–1964 (42D91)

Beaver & Co (Bingley) Ltd, worsted spinners: records 1885–1970 (47D91)

Sir James Hill & Sons Ltd, top makers, Keighley: records c1897-1988 (35D91)

John Robson (Shipley) Ltd, diesel engine mfrs: records 1903–88 (19D91)

National and Local Government Officers Association, Bingley branch: minutes 1923–61 (75D91)

WEST YORKSHIRE ARCHIVE SERVICE, CALDERDALE, CENTRAL LIBRARY, NORTHGATE HOUSE, NORTHGATE, HALIFAX HX1 1UN

William Edleston Ltd, woollen mfrs, Sowerby Bridge: records 1908–86 (WE)

Harper Garside, insurance brokers, Elland: records 1865–1970 (HGA)

Halifax Building Society: sealing registers 1936–77 (HXB)

Todmorden Industrial & Co-operative Society Ltd: records 1862–1976 (TC)

Halifax and District Post Office: records incl establishment books c1866–1963 (GPO)

WEST YORKSHIRE ARCHIVE SERVICE, KIRKLEES, CENTRAL LIBRARY, PRINCESS ALEXANDRA WALK, HUDDERSFIELD HD1 2SU

Ramsden family, baronets, of Byram (addnl): estate papers c1774–1913 (DD/RE)

Sykes family of Huddersfield, artists: papers c1880–1991 (KC520)

Douglas, Lawson & Co Ltd, pulley makers, Birstall: records c1880–1970 (KC488)

WC Holmes & Co Ltd, gas engineers, Huddersfield: records 1831–1981 (KC537)

Huddersfield and Holmfirth District Fire Brigade Friendly Society records 1932–89 (KC482)

WEST YORKSHIRE ARCHIVE SERVICE, LEEDS, CHAPELTOWN ROAD, SHEEPSCAR, LEEDS LS7 3AP

Chapman family of Fleet House, Wharfe: deeds and papers 1589–1932 (Acc 3591)

John Farrer & Co, estate agents, Oulton (addnl): records incl tithe maps 1769–1990 (Acc 3489)

Leeds and District Powerloom Overlookers Society records 1866–1991 (Acc 3570)

Pudsey Constituency Liberal Association minutes 1936–80 (Acc 3572)

Ripon Diocesan Readers Association records 1931–86 (Acc 3502)

Leeds Public Dispensary minutes 1824–1948 (Acc 3495)

WEST YORKSHIRE ARCHIVE SERVICE, YORKSHIRE ARCHAEOLOGICAL SOCIETY, CLAREMONT, 23 CLARENDON ROAD, LEEDS LS2 9NZ

Leeds Freemasons, Alfred lodge no 306: records 1795–20th cent (DD232)

Skelmanthorpe Wesleyan Day School records 1861–75 (DD235)

Local Repositories: Wales

CLWYD

CLWYD RECORD OFFICE, THE OLD
RECTORY, HAWARDEN,
DEESIDE CH5 3NR

Tyrell-Kenyon family, Barons Kenyon
of Gredington (addnl): deeds and estate
papers 13th–20th cent (D/KY)

Sir John Herbert Lewis MP (addnl):
corresp, diaries and papers c1860–1933
(D/L)

Old Marsh Farm, Sealand: corresp,
accounts and papers 1904–40
(D/DM/1107)

Institute of Building Control, North
Wales district: records 1976–91
(D/DM/1135)

National Union of Mineworkers,
Lancashire Cheshire and North Wales
Enginemen, Boilermen and Brakesmen's
Federation: corresp rel to employees in
North Wales 1947–65 (D/DM/1118)

National Union of Teachers, Flintshire
County Teachers Association: minutes
1903–74 (D/DM/1139)

Penyffordd (Holywell) Playing Fields
Association: records 1949–85
(D/DM/1129)

Rhyl and County Club records
1899–1971 (D/DM/1126)

Trevor Playing Fields Association,
Llanerch-y-môr: records 1939–68
(D/DM/1132)

Plans of abandoned non-coal mines,
Denbighshire and Flintshire 1826–1985
(AB)

ST DEINIOL'S LIBRARY, HAWARDEN

John Richard Humpidge Moorman
(1905–89), bishop of Ripon: research
notes rel to the Franciscan order

CLWYD RECORD OFFICE, 46 CLWYD
STREET, RUTHIN LL15 1HP

Daniel Jones, 'Professor Dan Leano',
entertainer: papers 1910–39
(DD/DM/973)

Powell Brothers Ltd, mechanical
engineers, Wrexham (addnl): accounts
and letter book 1909–26 (DD/DM/968)

National Union of Teachers,
Denbighshire County Teachers
Association: records 1952–74
(DD/DM/1007)

Wrexham Branch Co-operative Party:
minutes 1981–84 (DD/DM/964)

Rhyl and District Trades Council:
accounts, minutes and corresp 1943–60
(DD/DM/956)

Ancient Order of Foresters, Vale of
Clwyd court (addnl): records 1904–91
(DD/DM/970)

Denbigh and District Music Society:
minutes 1966–84 (DD/DM/956)

DYFED

DYFED ARCHIVE SERVICE,
CARMARTHENSHIRE RECORD OFFICE,
COUNTY HALL,
CARMARTHEN SA31 1JP

Pantglas estate: deeds and papers
18th–20th cent (Acc 6849)

Kidwelly-Pembrey Home Guard:
corresp 1941–42 (CDX 429)

DYFED ARCHIVE SERVICE,
PEMBROKESHIRE RECORD OFFICE,
THE CASTLE,
HAVERFORDWEST SA61 2EF

Owen family of Glogue: deeds and
papers incl rel to Glogue slate quarries
1856–1912 (HDX 1331)

GLAMORGAN
(MID AND SOUTH)

GLAMORGAN RECORD OFFICE,
COUNTY HALL, CATHAYS PARK,
CARDIFF CF1 3NE

Henry Samuel, Cardiff correspondent of the *Jewish Chronicle*: corresp and scrapbooks 1929–76 (D/D JR)

John Cory & Sons Ltd, shipowners, Cardiff: ledgers, minutes and papers 20th cent (D/D JC)

Wales Gas Consumers Council: records *c*1948–89 (D/D WGa)

National Union of Seamen, Cardiff branch: minute books 1927–72 (D/D NUS)

Glamorgan Surveyors Association minutes 1951–89 (D/D GSA)

Cardiff Womens Citizens Association (addnl): minute book 1929–45 (D/D X 675/1)

Association of Jewish Ex-Servicemen, Cardiff branch: corresp 1937–40 (D/D JR)

South Wales Tuberculosis Campaign Committee: papers 1952–66 (D/D X 675/2)

Contemporary Art Society for Wales: minutes and exhibition catalogues 1937–90 (D/D CASW)

Ynysybwl Workmens Hall: membership books and bingo account books 1937–82 (D/D X 667)

Penarth Council of Churches: minute books 1962–83 (D/D Pe CC)

Cardiff United Synagogue: minutes. corresp and reports *c*1950–89, and records incl burial books of Highfield Cemetery 1860–1970 (D/D JR)

Plans of abandoned non-coal mines 19th–20th cent (D/D HSE)

WEST GLAMORGAN

WEST GLAMORGAN RECORD
OFFICE, COUNTY HALL,
OYSTERMOUTH ROAD,
SWANSEA SA1 3SN

Neuadd estate, Brynamman: records rel to the Amman Iron Co and Cae Gurwen manor *c*1830–1950 (D/D SB)

Cory, Yeo & Co, Birchrock colliery, Pontardulais: records 19th cent (D/D SB)

John T Davies, chemist, Swansea: prescription books *c*1870–1950 (D/D Z)

Institute of Houseworkers, Swansea: records 1948–81

Afan Community Aid Council records *c*1980–89

Hebron Welsh Independent Chapel, Cymmer: register of members 1797–1859 (D/D Ind 5/1)

Swansea Free Church Council: minute books 1889–1982 (D/D FC 1/1–6)

List of Glamorgan freeholders 1744 (D/D Z 108)

Transferred from Port Talbot Library:

Log of the ship *Fidelity* 1847

St David's Unity of Ivorites, Caradoc ap Iestyn lodge: minutes 1864–1935

Aberavon and Port Talbot District Nurses Association: minutes 1898–1959

National Eisteddfod, Aberavon 1932: minutes

Port Talbot Pilotage Authority: records incl minutes and registers 1912–52

Records of Aberavon Borough, and Margam and Glyncorrwg urban district councils 1861–1960

GWENT

GWENT COUNTY RECORD OFFICE,
COUNTY HALL, CWMBRAN NP44 2XH

Watkins family of Wern-y-Cwm,
Llanvetherine: accounts books and
diaries 1757–1897 (Acc 2842)

Big Pit Colliery, Blaenafon (addnl):
records incl plans 19th–20th cent
(Accs 2891, 2903, 2921, 2943)

Pontypool Gas & Water Co (addnl):
ledgers, maps and plans 1878–1971;
Abersychan Gas Co records 1875–1913
(Acc 2852)

GWYNEDD

GWYNEDD ARCHIVES SERVICE,
CAERNARFON AREA RECORD OFFICE,
COUNTY OFFICES, SHIREHALL
STREET, CAERNARFON LL55 1SH

Reverend Thomas Morris, Pentrefelin:
papers 19th–20th cent (XD 89)

Welsh Water Authority records
1893–1989 (XD 93)

North Wales Advisory Council for
Technical Education: minutes 1943–48
(XEM 6)

North Wales Arts Association: files
c1960–89

Archive of Gwynedd Gardens: records
20th cent (XD 92)

GWYNEDD ARCHIVES SERVICE,
DOLGELLAU AREA RECORD OFFICE,
CAE PENARLAG, DOLGELLAU LL40 2YB

Dolgelley Social Club Co Ltd records
1901–78 (ZM 4255)

GWYNEDD ARCHIVES SERVICE,
LLANGEFNI AREA RECORD OFFICE,
SHIREHALL, LLANGEFNI LL77 7TW

WJ Jones 'Brynfab', Brynsiencyn:
lecture notes and minute books of
Undeb Gweithwyr Môn (Anglesey
Workers Union) 20th cent (WM 1400)

William Williams, Pentraeth and
Liverpool: notebooks rel to his
experiences in the Australian goldfields
19th cent (WM 1416)

Richard Jones, currier, Beaumaris:
records 19th cent (WDAAM)

POWYS

POWYS COUNTY ARCHIVES OFFICE,
COUNTY HALL,
LLANDRINDOD WELLS LD1 5LD

Dinas and Cantref Selyf manor court
leet and presentments book 1792–1801
(BX/24)

Thomas Jones, constable in
Montgomeryshire: journals 1843–48
(M/SOC/7)

Llandrindod Wells Golf Club records
1905–71; and Radnor Home Guard
papers 1940–57 (R/SOC/5)

Brecknock Museum: MS collection incl
Brecon Borough rent roll 1664;
Talachddu manor court leet book
1720–1865; Buckland estate books and
rentals 1780–1920; Wood family
political and personal papers 1806–1906,
incl lists of Glamorgan voters 1734–56
and Brecknock voters 1832–57; Brecon
Gas Co minutes 1855–1949

Local Repositories: Scotland

BORDERS

BORDERS REGION ARCHIVE AND
LOCAL HISTORY CENTRE, REGIONAL
LIBRARY HEADQUARTERS, ST MARY'S
MILL, SELKIRK TD7 5EW

Alexander Oliver (1827–1912), United
Presbyterian minister: autobiographical
memoranda (SC/R/67)

John Dodds, blacksmith, Gattonside:
account book 1847–51 (SC/R/66)

CENTRAL

CENTRAL REGIONAL COUNCIL
ARCHIVES DEPARTMENT, UNIT 6,
BURGHMUIR INDUSTRIAL ESTATE,
STIRLING FK7 7PY

Graham family of Callendar: deeds and
papers 1538–1637

Moir family of Leckie: deeds and papers
1527–1841

Braendam estate deeds 1701–1918
(PD103)

Major-General Sir David Bruce,
pathologist: personal career records
1881–1931

JG Stein & Co Ltd, refractory brick
makers, Bonnybridge: records
1882–1988

Alloa Masonic Lodge records 1757–1924
(PD106)

Balquhidder library, smithy and
ploughing society records 1853–1970
(PD107)

DUMFRIES AND GALLOWAY

DUMFRIES ARCHIVE CENTRE,
33 BURNS STREET, DUMFRIES DG12PS

Hugh Corrie, James Gilchrist, John
Maxwell and David Welsh, solicitors:
legal accounts and papers 1772–1819
(GGD 107)

Walter Newall, architect: corresp,
sketchbooks and drawings 1819–59
(GGD 130–31)

Scottish Girls Friendly Society,
Dumfries branch: minutes and corresp
1886–1917 (GGD 134)

Kirk session records of St Michael's
Church, Greyfriars Church and St
Mary's Church, Dumfries 1648–1964
(CH2/537, CH2/979, CH2/1049)
(transferred from the Scottish Record
Office)

GRAMPIAN

GRAMPIAN REGIONAL ARCHIVES,
OLD ABERDEEN HOUSE, DUNBAR
STREET, ABERDEEN AB2 1UE

Eleanor ME Berry (1898–1989): records
rel to her family history incl papers of
Walter Oliphant Berry (1827–1904),
and Edmund Berry (1855–1932), Danish
consul-generals in Edinburgh (PD [SRO
TD/90/30])

ABERDEEN CITY ARCHIVES, THE
CHARTER ROOM, THE TOWN HOUSE,
ABERDEEN AB9 1AQ

Scottish Salmon & White Fish Co Ltd,
wholesale fish merchants, Aberdeen:
minutes and accounts 1919–75 (Acc 70)

Aberdeen Chamber of Commerce:
records incl minutes c1853–1970
(Acc 74)

Convener Court and United Trades of
Old Aberdeen: records 1663–1940
(Acc 71)

St Nicholas, Aberdeen: kirk session
records 1562–1940

Aberdeen Customs and Excise records
1858–1970

HIGHLAND

HIGHLAND REGIONAL ARCHIVE,
INVERNESS BRANCH LIBRARY,
FARRALINE PARK,
INVERNESS IV1 1NH

Eddrachillis parish estate rental
1847–1922

Highland and Jacobite Exhibition:
minutes and papers 1903

Inverness Art Society records 1950–90

Inverness Field Club records 1875–1990

Northern Meeting: minutes, corresp
and accounts 1788–1957

LOTHIAN

CITY OF EDINBURGH DISTRICT
COUNCIL ARCHIVES,
DEPARTMENT OF ADMINISTRATION,
CITY CHAMBERS, HIGH STREET,
EDINBURGH EH1 1YJ

Association of Sworn Meters and
Weighers, Leith: records 1776–1989
(ECA 161)

Lothian and Borders Police Force:
records 1805–1980 (ECA 176)

STRATHCLYDE

STRATHCLYDE REGIONAL ARCHIVES,
MITCHELL LIBRARY, NORTH STREET,
GLASGOW G3 7DN

Mackenzie family of Dolphinton: deeds
and estate papers 1493–1960 (TD1231)
(transferred from the Scottish Record
Office)

Bird Semple & Crawford Herron,
solicitors, Glasgow: trust records
19th–20th cent (TD1197)

Fisher Ltd, marine engineers, Paisley:
records 20th cent (TD1201)

Mavor & Coulson Ltd, electrical and
mining machinery mfrs, Glasgow
(addnl): records 1891–1961 (TD279)

Newmilns Co-operative Society Ltd:
records 1889–1968 (TD1238)

Electrical Association for Women,
Glasgow and district branch: records
1953–87 (TD1229)

Scottish Co-operative Womens Guild,
Kinning Park branch: corresp and misc
papers 1902–79 (TD1206)

Scottish Steel Campaign records 1991
(TD1219)

Local Enterprise Advisory Project,
Glasgow: corresp 1975–82 (TD1210)

Milngavie Art Club records 1915–84
(TD1236)

Shipping registers for Ayr,
Campbeltown, Dumfries and Glasgow
1763–1890 (Acc 3889)

ARGYLL AND BUTE DISTRICT
ARCHIVES, KILMORY,
LOCHGILPHEAD PA31 8RT

MacTavish family of Dunardry: family
and estate papers 1650–1869

CITY OF GLASGOW, MITCHELL
LIBRARY, 201 NORTH STREET,
GLASGOW G3 7DN

Fleming family of Glasgow: papers incl
the Balmanno family 1619–1952
(Acc 891370)

Wingate, Birrell & Co, marine
insurance brokers and salvage agents,
Glasgow: private ledger 1973–86
(Acc 891353)

Scottish-Polish Society: records 20th
cent (Acc 891309)

Lieutenancy of Glasgow, lower ward of
Lanarkshire: minute book 1826–1931
(Acc 891369)

TAYSIDE

DUNDEE DISTRICT ARCHIVE AND
RECORD CENTRE, 14 CITY SQUARE,
DUNDEE DD1 3BY

Ogilvy family, baronets, of
Inverquharity: family and estate papers
c1665–1910

Ascreavie estate papers 1798–1875

PW Shearer, reporter and jute trade
expert: cuttings books and papers
1948–87

Andrew Mitchell & Stewart Ltd, sack
and bag mfrs, Dundee: travellers order
book 1907–11

Thow Bros, bagpipe makers and sack
printing block mfrs, Dundee: order
books, stamp books and accounts
c1873–1970

Junior Chamber, Dundee: records
c1960–85

Vehicle licensing registers for Angus
1903–74, Dundee 1904–81, Kinross-
shire 1904–54 and Perthshire 1909–11;
Kinross-shire drivers licensing register
1904–22

PERTH AND KINROSS DISTRICT
ARCHIVE, SANDEMAN LIBRARY,
16 KINNOULL STREET, PERTH PH1 5ET

Mitchell & Thomson, solicitors,
Comrie: letter books 1893–1974

J Pullar & Sons Ltd, dry cleaners and
dyers, Perth (addnl): records c1801–1990

J & D Smith & Co, linen drapers,
Perth: records c1900–73

Perthshire Art Association minutes
1924–84

Royal Strathearn Volunteers: fragments
of regimental order book 1805–07

Local Repositories: Isle of Man

MANX MUSEUM LIBRARY,
KINGSWOOD GROVE, DOUGLAS,
ISLE OF MAN

Douglas Dorcas Society (addnl): records
incl minutes 1891–1982 (Acc 8921)

II: Reports added to the National Register of Archives

The list notices Reports Nos 33457 to 34689 added to the National Register of Archives in 1991.

Appended is a short supplementary list of some of the more significant replacements and additions to existing reports received during the year.

Asterisks denote reports of which copies have been sent to the British Library (Official Publications Library), the Bodleian Library Oxford, the University Library Cambridge, London University Institute of Historical Research, the John Rylands University Library of Manchester, Birmingham Central Library, The Scottish Record Office, The National Library of Wales and The Queen's University Library, Belfast.

Nos 33457–34689

33457　Murray family of Touchadam and Polmaise: family and estate papers 265pp *Central Regional Council Archives Department*

33458　Dundee: St Mary's Parish Church 3pp *Dundee District Archive and Record Centre*

33459　Dundee: St Salvador's Episcopal Church 4pp *Dundee District Archive and Record Centre*

33460　Dundee Curling Club 6pp *Dundee District Archive and Record Centre*

33461　East Brothers Ltd, furniture mfrs, Dundee 5pp *Dundee District Archive and Record Centre*

33462　London: Scots Club 3pp *National Library of Scotland, Department of Manuscripts*

33463　Crook United Reformed Church 6pp *Durham County Record Office*

33464　Henry Robertson Bowers, polar explorer: corresp and papers 206pp *Cambridge University: Scott Polar Research Institute*

33465　Woodfield Cooke Ltd, chemists, Hoylake 1p *Wirral Archives Service*

33466　Lowndes family of Chesham: family and estate papers 129pp *Buckinghamshire Record Office*

33467　Birkenhead: St James' Hospital 1p *Wirral Archives Service*

33468　Birkenhead Young Mens Christian Association 3pp *Wirral Archives Service*

33469　Wirral Family Practitioner Committee 1p *Wirral Archives Service*

33470　Edward Hubbard, architectural historian: papers 9pp *Wirral Archives Service*

33471　Alison Bielski, poet: literary MSS and journals 14pp *National Library of Wales, Department of Manuscripts and Records*

33472　Lampard-Vachell family of Cardiff and Llantwit Major: deeds and papers 44pp *Glamorgan Record Office*

33473　Burbage Womens Institute 3pp *Wiltshire Record Office*

33474　Sherston Womens Institute 2pp *Wiltshire Record Office*

33475　TH White Ltd, agricultural engineers, Devizes 5pp *Wiltshire Record Office*

33476　Wiltshire County Bowling Association 1p *Wiltshire Record Office*

33477 Grace & Sons, monumental masons, Romsey 3pp *Hampshire Record Office*

33478 Wiltshire savings banks 7pp *Wiltshire Record Office*

33479 Imrie, Porter & Wakefield, architects, Warminster 14pp *Wiltshire Record Office*

33480 Wiltshire Community Council 9pp *Wiltshire Record Office*

33481 Hilperton Housing Association Ltd 2pp *Wiltshire Record Office*

33482 Bellairs family: corresp and papers 6pp *Hampshire Record Office*

33483 Ashton Keynes Congregational Church 1p *Wiltshire Record Office*

33484 Swindon: Immanuel United Reformed Church 7pp *Wiltshire Record Office*

33485 Mid-Wiltshire Methodist Circuit 10pp *Wiltshire Record Office*

33486 Trowbridge: Yerbury Widows' Almshouses 4pp *Wiltshire Record Office*

33487 Manaos Tramways & Light Co Ltd, London 6pp *Guildhall Library*

33488 WH Tindall & Co, tea and coffee importers and general merchants, London 9pp *Guildhall Library*

33489 British Rail, London Midland and Western Regions and predecessor bodies 8pp *Cheshire Record Office*

33490 Broughton Baptist Church 8pp *Oxford University: Regents Park College, Angus Library*

33491 Hemel Hempstead: Carey Baptist Church 5pp *Oxford University: Regents Park College, Angus Library*

33492 William Carey, missionary: family letters 22pp *Oxford University: Regents Park College, Angus Library*

33493 John Saffery, Baptist minister: corresp 24pp *Oxford University: Regents Park College, Angus Library*

33494 Particular Baptist Fund 12pp *Oxford University: Regents Park College, Angus Library*

33495 Whitchurch Baptist Church 2pp *Oxford University: Regents Park College, Angus Library*

33496 Oxton Friendly Bovial Society 1p *Borders Region Archive and Local History Centre*

33497 Leitholm and District Nursing Association 51pp *Borders Region Archive and Local History Centre*

33498 Baptist Union: MS collections 20pp *Oxford University: Regents Park College, Angus Library*

33499 Bootle: St Paul's and Trinity United Reformed Church 6pp *Merseyside Record Office*

33500 Runcorn shipping registration papers 7pp *Cheshire Record Office*

33501 Widnes: Milton United Reformed Church 8pp *Merseyside Record Office*

33502 Birkenhead: Grange Road Baptist Church 2pp *Merseyside Record Office*

33503 Merseyside Baptist District 1p *Merseyside Record Office*

33504 Waterloo Methodist Church 2pp *Merseyside Record Office*

33505 Birkenhead: Trinity Presbyterian Church 5pp *Merseyside Record Office*

33506 Merseyside and West Cheshire Area Citizens Advice Bureaux 7pp *Merseyside Record Office*

33507 Liverpool: Walton Hospital 9pp *Merseyside Record Office*

33508 Waterloo and District General Hospital 3pp *Merseyside Record Office*

33509 Merseyside coroners' records 14pp *Merseyside Record Office*

33510 Trelawny family of Ham: corresp and papers 2pp *West Devon Area Record Office*

33511 Edrica De La Pole, dog breeder and farmer: diaries and papers 3pp *West Devon Area Record Office*

33512 Liverpool Corporation Waterworks 3pp *Merseyside Record Office*

33513 HA Noel Woodall, architect, Liverpool 25pp *Merseyside Record Office*

33514 Tom Mann, trade unionist and communist: corresp and papers 8pp *Coventry Central Library*

33515 Aberystwyth and District Citizens Advice Bureau 6pp *Dyfed Archives Service, Cardiganshire Area Record Office*

33516 Blandy & Blandy, solicitors, Reading: clients papers 80pp *Berkshire Record Office*

33517 DSR Williams, solicitor, Lampeter: deeds and clients papers 29pp *Dyfed Archives Service, Cardiganshire Area Record Office*

33518 Aberystwyth: King's Hall 41pp *Dyfed Archives Service, Cardiganshire Area Record Office*

33519 Courage Ltd, brewers, London: Berkshire public house deeds 165pp *Berkshire Record Office*

33520 Bridge End Foundry Co Ltd, Cardigan: motor agency records 22pp *Dyfed Archives Service, Cardiganshire Area Record Office*

33521 JP Baillie, civil engineer: business and personal corresp and papers 7pp *Dyfed Archives Service, Cardiganshire Area Record Office*

33522 Meikle family, millwrights, Dunbar 7pp *Private*

33523 Sir Benjamin Heath Malkin, supreme court judge, Calcutta: corresp 8pp *Oriental and India Office Collections*

33524 Friends of Vellore in the United Kingdom and Ireland 38pp *Oriental and India Office Collections*

33525 Indian Police Collection 67pp *Oriental and India Office Collections*

33526 Palmer family, Earls of Selborne: estate papers 4pp *Reading University: Institute of Agricultural History and Museum of English Rural Life*

33527 Caernarfon Liberal Club 3pp *Gwynedd Archives and Museums Service, Caernarfon Area Record Office*

33528 Sarn District Nursing Association 2pp *Gwynedd Archives and Museums Service, Caernarfon Area Record Office*

33529 Bangor and District Society for Mentally Handicapped Children 4pp *Gwynedd Archives and Museums Service, Caernarfon Area Record Office*

33530 Upper Llanddeiniolen District Nursing Association 1p *Gwynedd Archives and Museums Service, Caernarfon Area Record Office*

33531 North Wales Society for the Blind 2pp *Gwynedd Archives and Museums Service, Caernarfon Area Record Office*

33532 Betws Garmon: Capel Salem 2pp *Gwynedd Archives and Museums Service, Caernarfon Area Record Office*

33533 Griffith Griffiths, shopkeeper and chemist, Llangwnadl 1p *Gwynedd Archives and Museums Service, Caernarfon Area Record Office*

33534 Llanberis District Nursing Association 1p *Gwynedd Archives and Museums Service, Caernarfon Area Record Office*

33535 Richard Jones, printer and bookseller, Pwllheli 1p *Gwynedd Archives and Museums Service, Caernarfon Area Record Office*

33536 Rowen Womens Institute 2pp *Gwynedd Archives and Museums Service, Caernarfon Area Record Office*

33537 William Rowlands & Co (Bangor) Ltd, wine and spirit merchants, Caernarfon 9pp *Gwynedd Archives and Museums Service, Caernarfon Area Record Office*

33538 Cwm-y-Glo: Barachiah Calvinistic Methodist Chapel 3pp *Gwynedd Archives and Museums Service, Caernarfon Area Record Office*

33539 H Pugh Jones, grocer, Cricieth 1p *Gwynedd Archives and Museums Service, Caernarfon Area Record Office*

33540 Rowlands family of Bethesda: letters from family members in the USA 12pp *Gwynedd Archives and Museums Service, Caernarfon Area Record Office*

33541 Bontnewydd Womens Voluntary Service 1p *Gwynedd Archives and Museums Service, Caernarfon Area Record Office*

33542 Caernarvonshire Home Guard, 3rd Battalion 6pp *Gwynedd Archives and Museums Service, Caernarfon Area Record Office*

33543 Richard Davies, builder and contractor, Caernarfon 1p *Gwynedd Archives and Museums Service, Caernarfon Area Record Office*

33544 Caernarvon Trades and Labour Council 3pp *Gwynedd Archives and Museums Service, Caernarfon Area Record Office*

33545 Thynne family, Barons Carteret: Beds estate papers 120pp *Bedfordshire Record Office*

33546 Jack Common, writer: corresp and papers 18pp *University of Newcastle upon Tyne: Robinson Library*

33547 Kenneth Frank Bowden, oceanographer: research diaries 3pp *Liverpool University Archives Unit*

33548 RH Thomas, grocer, Caernarfon 2pp *Gwynedd Archives and Museums Service, Caernarfon Area Record Office*

33549 Charles Dickens, novelist: corresp and literary papers[1] 285pp *University of Texas at Austin: Humanities Research Center*

33550 Jane Oliver, writer: corresp and papers 25pp *Borders Region Archive and Local History Centre*

33551 EC Theedam Ltd, sheet metal workers and ironmongers, Dudley 1p *Dudley Archives and Local History Department*

33552 Isaiah Woodall & Sons Ltd, engineers and hearth furniture mfrs, Dudley 2pp *Dudley Archives and Local History Department*

33553 Penllyn Calvinistic Methodist sunday schools 1p *Gwynedd Archives and Museums Service, Caernarfon Area Record Office*

33554 Pwllheli: Morgan Ambulance Committee 4pp *Gwynedd Archives and Museums Service, Caernarfon Area Record Office*

33555 Portmadoc: St John Ambulance Association and Brigade 1p *Gwynedd Archives and Museums Service, Caernarfon Area Record Office*

33556 Portmadoc: sub-commissioners of pilotage 1p *Gwynedd Archives and Museums Service, Caernarfon Area Record Office*

33557 Eliot Crawshay-Williams MP, poet and novelist: family, political and literary corresp and papers 110pp *National Library of Wales, Department of Manuscripts and Records*

33558 Holyhead Urban District Council 7pp *Gwynedd Archives and Museums Service, Llangefni Area Record Office*

33559 Llangoed Calvinistic Methodist Chapel 4pp *Gwynedd Archives and Museums Service, Llangefni Area Record Office*

33560 Jones & Lloyd Ltd, chain and anchor mfrs, Cradley 9pp *Dudley Archives and Local History Department*

33561 Anglesey County Nursing Association 18pp *Gwynedd Archives and Museums Service, Llangefni Area Record Office*

33562 Union Grinding Wheel Co, Sheffield 2pp *Sheffield Archives*

33563 Royal National Lifeboat Institution: Anglesey branch 70pp *Gwynedd Archives and Museums Service, Llangefni Area Record Office*

33564 Alfred Dutton, paymaster of HMS Tara: corresp and papers 15pp *Gwynedd Archives and Museums Service, Llangefni Area Record Office*

33565 H Hughes & Son Ltd, ironmongers, Llanerchymedd 14pp *Gwynedd Archives and Museums Service, Llangefni Area Record Office*

33566 Bulkeley Arms Hotel, Beaumaris 29pp *Gwynedd Archives and Museums Service, Llangefni Area Record Office*

33567 Actresses Franchise League 3pp *Fawcett Library*

33568 Anglesey County Constabulary 22pp *Gwynedd Archives and Museums Service, Llangefni Area Record Office*

33569 Womens Publicity Planning Association 10pp *Fawcett Library*

33570 National Womens Register 5pp *Fawcett Library*

33571 Anglican Group for the Ordination of Women to the Historic Ministry of the Church 4pp *Fawcett Library*

33572 Bangor and Beaumaris Board of Guardians 118pp *Gwynedd Archives and Museums Service, Llangefni Area Record Office*

---

[1]Sister Lucile Carr: *A Catalogue of the Vanderpoel Dickens Collection at the University of Texas,* 1968

33573 A Muriel Pierotti, feminist and trade unionist: corresp and papers 37pp *Fawcett Library*

33574 Anglesey and Holyhead boards of guardians 128pp *Gwynedd Archives and Museums Service, Llangefni Area Record Office*

33575 Anglesey parishes 74pp *Gwynedd Archives and Museums Service, Llangefni Area Record Office*

33576 Lyons Tetley Ltd, tea and coffee blenders, Greenford 68pp *Private*

33577 Charity Commission: Anglesey charities accounts 19pp *Gwynedd Archives and Museums Service, Llangefni Area Record Office*

33578 Laporte plc, chemical mfrs, London 225pp *Private*

33579 Winsford: Brunner Guildhall 1p *Cheshire Record Office*

33580 Anglesey Savings Bank 47pp *Gwynedd Archives and Museums Service, Llangefni Area Record Office*

33581 Amlwch and Holyhead English Wesleyan Methodist chapels 9pp *Gwynedd Archives and Museums Service, Llangefni Area Record Office*

33582 Menai Bridge Pier 32pp *Gwynedd Archives and Museums Service, Llangefni Area Record Office*

33583 M & W Grazebrook Ltd, engineers and boiler makers, Netherton 2pp *Dudley Archives and Local History Department*

33584 Archibald Kenrick & Sons Ltd, hardware and hollow-ware mfrs, West Bromwich 16pp *Private*

33585 Clifton Suspension Bridge Co, Bristol 8pp *Bristol University Library*

33586 Conwy Lloyd Morgan, comparative psychologist and philosopher: corresp and papers 23pp *Bristol University Library*

33587 Hamish Hamilton Ltd, publishers, London 36pp *Bristol University Library*

33588 David James Cathcart King, writer on castles: corresp and papers 8pp *Bristol University Library*

33589 Snead-Cox family of Broxwood: family and estate papers 10pp *Hereford Record Office*

33590 Bere Regis, Pimperne, Milton, and Milton and Blandford rural deaneries 3pp *Dorset Record Office*

33591 Beaminster Rural Deanery 1p *Dorset Record Office*

33592 Lyme Bay Rural Deanery 2pp *Dorset Record Office*

33593 Clapham: Annie McCall Maternity Hospital 3pp *Greater London Record Office and History Library*

33594 Newington Barrow alias Highbury manor records 8pp *Greater London Record Office and History Library*

33595 Business Equipment Trade Association 7pp *Greater London Record Office and History Library*

33596 London Council of Social Service 128pp *Greater London Record Office and History Library*

33597 London Labour Party 156pp *Greater London Record Office and History Library*

33598 Smith Kendon Ltd, manufacturing chemists and confectioners, Southwark 36pp *Greater London Record Office and History Library*

33599 Yale & Hardcastle, surveyors and estate agents, Caernarfon 62pp *Gwynedd Archives and Museums Service, Llangefni Area Record Office*

33600 North Eastern Electricity Board 71pp *Tyne and Wear Archives Service*

33601 T Fanning Evans, mine agent, Amlwch: business and personal papers 23pp *Gwynedd Archives and Museums Service, Llangefni Area Record Office*

33602 Newcastle upon Tyne: Princess Mary Maternity Hospital 18pp *Tyne and Wear Archives Service*

33603 Newcastle upon Tyne: Church of the Divine Unity 59pp *Tyne and Wear Archives Service*

33604 Amalgamated Union of Engineering Workers, Engineering Section 13pp *Warwick University Modern Records Centre*

33605 Lloyd family of Plas Tregayan, Anglesey and Aberdunant, Caernarfonshire: estate papers 41pp *Gwynedd Archives and Museums Service, Llangefni Area Record Office*

33606 Dinmor Park Quarry, limestone quarry, Penmon 14pp *Gwynedd Archives and Museums Service, Llangefni Area Record Office*

33607 Wilkinson Sword Ltd, sword and gun makers, London 4pp *Private*

33608 Washington Urban District Council 32pp *Tyne and Wear Archives Service*

33609 Gosforth Urban District Council 60pp *Tyne and Wear Archives Service*

33610 Anglesey registers of duties on land values and land tax assessments 96pp *Gwynedd Archives and Museums Service, Llangefni Area Record Office*

33611 Anglesey eisteddfodau 42pp *Gwynedd Archives and Museums Service, Llangefni Area Record Office*

33612 Garway Baptist Church 2pp *Hereford Record Office*

33613 Coliseum Cinema, Aberystwyth 16pp *Dyfed Archives Service, Cardiganshire Area Record Office*

33614 Newcastle upon Tyne: Company of Shipwrights 2pp *Tyne and Wear Archives Service*

33615 Cambrian News, newspaper, Aberystwyth 1p *Dyfed Archives Service, Cardiganshire Area Record Office*

33616 Leicestershire Miners Association 1p *Leicestershire Record Office*

33617 Hereford City Nursing and Maternity Society 2pp *Hereford Record Office*

33618 National Farmers Union: Herefordshire branch 11pp *Hereford Record Office*

33619 Hereford Rescue and Protection Society 3pp *Hereford Record Office*

33620 Lord Scudamore's Trust: records of the endowed schools 2pp *Hereford Record Office*

33621 Samuel William Clowes MP: Quorn Hunt papers 2pp *Leicestershire Record Office*

33622 IDE Elias, solicitor, Llandeilo: clients papers 39pp *Dyfed Archives Service, Carmarthenshire Area Record Office*

33623 Morris, Lloyd & Griffiths, solicitors, Carmarthen: deeds 27pp *Dyfed Archives Service, Carmarthenshire Area Record Office*

33624 Lewis family of New House: deeds and estate papers 123pp *Glamorgan Record Office*

33625 Washington Development Corporation 3pp *Tyne and Wear Archives Service*

33626 Amphlett, Lewis & Evans, solicitors, Llandysul: deeds 31pp *Dyfed Archives Service, Carmarthenshire Area Record Office*

33627 Thomas Giordani Wright, physician: diaries 2pp *Tyne and Wear Archives Service*

33628 Hetton United Methodist Circuit 2pp *Tyne and Wear Archives Service*

33629 Hetton Methodist Circuit 5pp *Tyne and Wear Archives Service*

33630 John Hamilton Howell, farmer, Trewellwell, Solva 16pp *Dyfed Archives Service, Carmarthenshire Area Record Office*

*33631 Sir Victor Horsley, physiologist and surgeon: personal and family papers 41pp *London University: University College Manuscripts Room*

33632 Lewis-Philipps family of Clyngwynne, Llanboidy: deeds and misc family papers 51pp *Dyfed Archives Service, Carmarthenshire Area Record Office*

33633 Associated Society of Locomotive Engineers and Firemen: Carmarthen branch 4pp *Dyfed Archives Service, Carmarthenshire Area Record Office*

33634 Goodwin Barsby & Co Ltd, quarry plant mfrs, Leicester 5pp *Leicestershire Record Office*

33635 Leicestershire Baptist marriage registers 8pp *Leicestershire Record Office*

33636 Thurlaston General Baptist Church 1p *Leicestershire Record Office*

33637 Market Harborough Urban District Council 2pp *Leicestershire Record Office*

33638 Rutland County Council 2pp *Leicestershire Record Office*

33639 Maldon shipping registers 8pp *Essex Record Office*

33640 Walbro Cycle & Motor Co, motor cycle agents, Saffron Walden 2pp *Essex Record Office*

33641 Brentwood Baptist Church 16pp *Essex Record Office*

33642 Little Waltham United Reformed Church 8pp *Essex Record Office*

33643 Southend-on-Sea Baptist Church 3pp *Essex Record Office, Southend Branch*

33644 Pitsea Baptist Church 2pp *Essex Record Office, Southend Branch*

33645 Rayleigh Congregational Church 3pp *Essex Record Office, Southend Branch*

33646 Southend-on-Sea Teachers Association 10pp *Essex Record Office, Southend Branch*

33647 Tottenham: St Ann's Hospital 1p *Greater London Record Office and History Library*

33648 South London Hospital for Women and Children 51pp *Greater London Record Office and History Library*

33649 Vehicle & General Insurance Co Ltd: records incl liquidators papers 19pp *Greater London Record Office and History Library*

33650 Caterham: St Lawrence's Hospital 38pp *Greater London Office and History Library*

33651 Southend Unitarian Meeting House 8pp *Essex Record Office, Southend Branch*

33652 Ramsden Bellhouse Womens Institute 4pp *Essex Record Office*

33653 Elizabeth Garrett Anderson Hospital Staff Action Committee 16pp *Greater London Record Office and History Library*

33654 Episcopal Church in Scotland: Glasgow and Galloway Diocese congregations 300pp *Private*

33655 United Patternmakers Association: Aberdeen, Glasgow, Kilmarnock, Partick and Renfrew branches 3pp *Strathclyde Regional Archives*

33656 Mary Augusta Ward, novelist and social worker: corresp and literary papers 11pp *Pusey House Library*

33657 Mary Augusta Ward, novelist and social worker: corresp and literary papers 1p *Claremont Colleges: Honnold Library*

33658 Mary Augusta Ward, novelist and social worker: corresp and papers 1p *Private*

33659 Southampton Chamber of Commerce 3pp *Southampton City Records Office*

33660 Arbroath: Dale Cottage Industrial School 2pp *Dundee District Archive and Record Centre*

33661 Tullis Russell & Co Ltd, paper mfrs, Markinch 31pp *Private*

33662 Egerton family, Earls of Wilton and Viscounts Grey de Wilton: Batley estate papers 32pp *West Yorkshire Archive Service, Yorkshire Archaeological Society*

33663 TP & JL Low, solicitors, Kirkwall: clients papers 13pp *Orkney Archives*

33664 Thoms bequest for the restoration of St Magnus Cathedral, Kirkwall 4pp *Orkney Archives*

33665 Educational Institute of Scotland: Orkney branch 3pp *Orkney Archives*

33666 Aberdeen City Archives: misc accessions 4pp *Aberdeen City Archives*

33667 Camberwell, Peckham and Dulwich Free Church Council 1p *Lambeth Archives Department*

33668 Clapham Liberal Association 2pp *Lambeth Archives Department*

33669 Lambeth Central Labour Party 5pp *Lambeth Archives Department*

33670 Truman, Hanbury, Buxton & Co Ltd: South London public house deeds 5pp *Lambeth Archives Department*

33671 Clapham Athenaeum 1p *Lambeth Archives Department*

33672 HW Nevill Ltd, bread mfrs, Herne Hill 11pp *Lambeth Archives Department*

33673 Deane & Co, chemists, Clapham 1p *Lambeth Archives Department*

33674 Loughborough Junction Maternity and Child Welfare Centre, Brixton 1p *Lambeth Archives Department*

33675 National Savings Movement: Lambeth committee 1p *Lambeth Archives Department*

33676 John E Rowling, dairyman, Lambeth 4pp *Lambeth Archives Department*

33677 Lambeth & Southwark Housing Society Ltd 4pp *Lambeth Archives Department*

33678 Brixton District Nursing Association 4pp *Lambeth Archives Department*

33679 Lambeth Pension Society 1p *Lambeth Archives Department*

33680 Lambeth Savings Bank 1p *Lambeth Archives Department*

33681 Upper Norwood Athenaeum 2pp *Lambeth Archives Department*

33682 C Copus & Sons, furnishing undertakers, Clapham 1p *Lambeth Archives Department*

33683 1st Surrey Rifles 11pp *Lambeth Archives Department*

33684 Brixton: Friendly Almshouses 3pp *Lambeth Archives Department*

33685 Lambeth charities 12pp *Lambeth Archives Department*

33686 Sandbach family of Hafodunos and Bryngwyn: family and estate papers 87pp *Powys County Archives Office*

33687 Lazar Zaidman, communist and Jewish activist: corresp and papers 31pp *Sheffield University Library*

33688 Webster & Horsfall Ltd, spring steel wire mfrs, Birmingham 10pp *Private*

33689 Lambeth Methodist Circuit 8pp *Lambeth Archives Department*

33690 Brixton: Mostyn Road Methodist Church 2pp *Lambeth Archives Department*

33691 Streatham: Magdalen Hospital Classifying School for Girls 5pp *Lambeth Archives Department*

33692 Streatham Antiquarian Society 49pp *Lambeth Archives Department*

33693 Henry Lewis Doulton, industrialist: deeds and estate papers 22pp *Lambeth Archives Department*

33694 James Colvill, nurseryman, Chelsea 9pp *Lambeth Archives Department*

33695 Henry Benjamin Hanbury Beaufoy, benefactor: corresp rel to foundation of Lambeth Ragged School 34pp *Lambeth Archives Department*

33696 Lambeth Estate Co Ltd 2pp *Lambeth Archives Department*

33697 Lambeth Archives Department: misc accessions 131pp *Lambeth Archives Department*

33698 Bourne-Arton family of Tanfield Lodge: papers, incl estate papers of the Brudenell-Bruce family, Marquesses of Ailesbury 76pp *North Yorkshire County Record Office*

33699 Holcombe Rogus manor records 4pp *Devon Record Office*

33700 National Women Citizens Association 72pp *Fawcett Library*

33701 National Union of Womens Suffrage Societies 16pp *Fawcett Library*

33702 National Union of Societies for Equal Citizenship 23pp *Fawcett Library*

33703 Gloucester United Reformed Church 6pp *Gloucestershire Record Office*

33704 Southend District Coroners 2pp *Essex Record Office, Southend Branch*

33705 Denbighshire Quarter Sessions 404pp *Clwyd Record Office,*[1] *Ruthin Branch*

33706 Berkeley Burial Committee 7pp *Gloucestershire Record Office*

33707 Macclesfield and District Citizens Advice Bureau 2pp *Cheshire Record Office*

33708 Crewe Borough Petty Sessions 3pp *Cheshire Record Office*

33709 Nantwich Petty Sessions 2pp *Cheshire Record Office*

33710 Vincent Morris & Co Ltd, drapers, Llanelli 2pp *Dyfed Archives Service, Carmarthenshire Area Record Office*

33711 Mid-Cheshire (Knutsford) Farmers Association Show Society 2pp *Cheshire Record Office*

---

[1] AG Veysey (ed): *A Handlist of the Denbighshire Quarter Sessions Records vols 1-11,* 1991

33712 Chester, Wrexham & District Savings Bank: Knutsford branch 2pp *Cheshire Record Office*

33713 Carmarthen Borough 1p *Dyfed Archives Service, Carmarthenshire Area Record Office*

33714 John Paul Rylands, barrister and genealogist: notebooks and papers 4pp *Cheshire Record Office*

33715 Preseli Pembrokeshire District Council 10pp *Dyfed Archives Service, Pembrokeshire Area Record Office*

33716 Phyllis Helen Bodley: memoir of her husband John Edward Courtenay Bodley, civil servant and historian, incl original corresp 11pp *Oxford University: Balliol College Library*

33717 Atkins-Bowyer family of Steeple Aston: Manor estate papers 2pp *Lambeth Archives Department*

33718 Lambeth Church Committee of Social Service 1p *Lambeth Archives Department*

33719 Samuel Pearce Carey, biographer: papers incl Carey and Pearce family letters 8pp *Oxford University: Regents Park College, Angus Library*

33720 Vice-Admiral Sir Thomas Masterman Hardy, 1st Bt: letters to Edward Thorne 5pp *Portsmouth City Records Office*

33721 National and Local Government Officers Association: Portsmouth branch 3pp *Portsmouth City Records Office*

33722 Portsmouth and District Natural History Society 2pp *Portsmouth City Records Office*

33723 Southern Unitarian Association 1p *Portsmouth City Records Office*

33724 Portsmouth Methodist churches and circuits 69pp *Portsmouth City Records Office*

33725 Portsmouth Central Library: MS collections 40pp *Portsmouth City Records Office*

33726 Hereford Training College for Teachers: Old Students Guild 4pp *Hereford Record Office*

33727 Sutton Housing Trust 20pp *Greater London Record Office and History Library*

33728 Stratford-on-Avon Methodist Circuit 4pp *Shakespeare Birthplace Trust Records Office*

33729 Walter Crane, artist and designer: corresp and papers 32pp *Royal Borough of Kensington and Chelsea Libraries and Arts Service, Kensington*

33730 Salford East Constituency Labour Party 2pp *Salford Archives Centre*

33731 Salford West Constituency Labour Party 1p *Salford Archives Centre*

33732 Tyldesley Coal Co Ltd 2pp *Salford Archives Centre*

33733 National Union of Mineworkers, Lancashire area: Cronton branch 13pp *Salford Museum of Mining*

33734 Charlestown Congregational Church 4pp *Salford Archives Centre*

33735 Swinton Unitarian Free Church 8pp *Salford Archives Centre*

33736 North Western Co-operative Music Association 2pp *Salford Archives Centre*

33737 Charles Craib Middleton, chemical engineer: corresp and working papers 16pp *Salford Archives Centre*

33738 Eccles and District History Society 4pp *Salford Archives Centre*

33739 JO Grant & Co Ltd, timber merchants and joinery mfrs, Salford 7pp *Salford Archives Centre*

33740 Worsley and District Trades Council 3pp *Salford Archives Centre*

33741 Thomas Reynolds Senior & Sons Ltd, musical instrument mfrs and dealers, Salford 2pp *Salford Archives Centre*

33742 Order of the Sons of Temperance Friendly Society: Salford Grand Division no 8 2pp *Salford Archives Centre*

33743 Nasmyth, Wilson & Co Ltd, locomotive, hydraulic and general engineers, Salford 37pp *Salford Archives Centre*

33744 Barker & Swift (Manufacturers) Ltd, cotton mfrs, Pendlebury 3pp *Salford Archives Centre*

33745 Irlam and Cadishead Welfare and Aftercare Association 3pp *Salford Archives Centre*

33746 Sir Peter Maxwell Davies, composer and conductor: notes and scores 12pp *Salford Archives Centre*

33747 James Nasmyth, engineer: collected corresp and papers 13pp *Salford Archives Centre*

33748 Electrical Association for Women: Eccles and district branch 1p *Salford Archives Centre*

33749 Manchester Racecourse Co Ltd 2pp *Salford Archives Centre*

33750 Eccles Citizens Advice Bureau 1p *Salford Archives Centre*

33751 Worsley Citizens Advice Bureau 1p *Salford Archives Centre*

33752 Lower Broughton Citizens Advice Bureau 1p *Salford Archives Centre*

33753 East Devon District Council 4pp *Devon Record Office*

33754 Buckfastleigh United Reformed Church 4pp *Devon Record Office*

33755 Reynell family of Forde House: family and estate papers 37pp *Devon Record Office*

33756 Exeter: Feoffees of St Sidwell 27pp *Devon Record Office*

33757 Bromhead (Bristol) Ltd, photographers 1p *Bristol Record Office*

33758 CJ King & Sons (Holdings) Ltd, stevedores and tug owners, Avonmouth 45pp *Bristol Record Office*

33759 Bristol: St Mary's on the Quay Roman Catholic Church 9pp *Bristol Record Office*

33760 Webley & Scott Ltd, gun and pistol makers, Birmingham 10pp *Private*

33761 Carmarthen Museum: MS collections 31pp *Dyfed Archives Service, Carmarthenshire Area Record Office*

33762 Wentworth-Fitzwilliam family, Earls Fitzwilliam: estate papers 49pp *North Yorkshire County Record Office*

33763 London Hospital Medical Club 5pp *Royal London Hospital Archives Centre and Museum*

33764 National Liberal Club 450pp *Bristol University Library*

33765 Kate Roberts, novelist, short-story writer and literary journalist: corresp and papers 349pp *National Library of Wales, Department of Manuscripts and Records*

*33766 Sir Charles Maurice Yonge, marine biologist: corresp and papers 95pp *Natural History Museum*

33767 Broughton-in-Furness manor records 160pp *Cumbria Record Office, Barrow*

*33768 CS Lewis, writer and scholar: corresp and literary papers 57pp *Oxford University: Bodleian Library, Department of Western Manuscripts*

33769 John Watson, publican, landlord and property tax collector: papers 17pp *Sandwell District Libraries*

33770 Chester Petty Sessions 7pp *Chester City Record Office*

33771 Chester: Rows Research Project 5pp *Chester City Record Office*

33772 London University, University College: James Joyce Centre archives 11pp *London University: University College Manuscripts Room*

33773 Sir William Maddock Bayliss and Leonard Ernest Bayliss, physiologists: corresp and papers 12pp *London University: University College Manuscripts Room*

33774 William Paton Ker, scholar and author: corresp and papers 7pp *London University: University College Manuscripts Room*

33775 Mark (Max) Plowman, writer and pacifist: corresp and papers 6pp *London University: University College Manuscripts Room*

33776 Bank of London & South America Ltd 62pp *London University: University College Manuscripts Room*

33777 Lionel Felix Gilbert, chemist: corresp and papers rel to biography of WH Wollaston 30pp *London University: University College Manuscripts Room*

33778 WJ Sutton Ltd, manufacturing jewellers, Birmingham 6pp *Private*

33779 Methodist Archives and Research Centre: misc accessions 28pp *Manchester University: Methodist Archives and Research Centre*

33780 GF Lodder & Sons, solicitors, Henley-in-Arden: deeds and papers 38pp *Shakespeare Birthplace Trust Records Office*

33781 Archer family, Barons Archer and Musgrave family: deeds and papers 36pp *Shakespeare Birthplace Trust Records Office*

33782 Exeter Law Library Society 2pp *Devon Record Office*

33783 Exeter: South Street Baptist Church 1p *Devon Record Office*

33784 Richard Cresswell, vicar of Salcombe Regis and Beatrix F Cresswell: diaries 1p *Devon Record Office*

33785 Devon Area Health Authority 2pp *Devon Record Office*

33786 National Union of Journalists: Halifax branch 6pp *West Yorkshire Archive Service, Calderdale*

33787 Amalgamated Union of Engineering Workers: Brighouse branch 6pp *West Yorkshire Archive Service, Calderdale*

33788 National Union of Dyers, Bleachers and Textile Workers: Brighouse Dyers branch 4pp *West Yorkshire Archive Service, Calderdale*

33789 Amalgamated Society of Boilermakers, Shipwrights, Blacksmiths and Structural Workers: Halifax branch 2pp *West Yorkshire Archive Service, Calderdale*

33790 George Rolleston, physician: corresp 7pp *Wellcome Institute for the History of Medicine*

33791 Sir John Bowring, writer and diplomat: corresp and papers 4pp *Wellcome Institute for the History of Medicine*

33792 Sir George Newman, public health reformer: corresp 25pp *Wellcome Institute for the History of Medicine*

33793 Scottish Agricultural Arbiters Association 7pp *Private*

33794 Royal Scottish Automobile Club 9pp *Strathclyde Regional Archives*

33795 Queens Nursing Institute, Scotland 10pp *Private*

33796 Moir family of Leckie: deeds and papers 7pp *Central Regional Council Archives Department*

33797 British Clothing Industry Association: records of predecessor bodies 1p *Warwick University Modern Records Centre*

33798 National Union of Teachers 4pp *Warwick University Modern Records Centre*

33799 Transport and General Workers Union: Yorkshire glass bottle industry 8pp *Warwick University Modern Records Centre*

33800 EJ Rawlins & Co Ltd, paint mfrs, Leeds 5pp *West Yorkshire Archive Service, Leeds*

33801 George Bray & Co Ltd, gas burner and electrical appliance mfrs, Leeds 16pp *West Yorkshire Archive Service, Leeds*

33802 Frederick Dyson & Sons Ltd, ironfounders, Leeds 2pp *West Yorkshire Archive Service, Leeds*

33803 Harding (Leeds) Ltd, textile pin and machinery accessory mfrs 18pp *West Yorkshire Archive Service, Leeds*

33804 Leeds (Richmond Hill) Methodist Circuit 14pp *West Yorkshire Archive Service, Leeds*

33805 Leeds (Lady Lane) Methodist Circuit 2pp *West Yorkshire Archive Service, Leeds*

33806 Drighlington Congregational Church 3pp West Yorkshire Archive Service, Leeds

33807 Leeds: St Andrews United Reformed Church, Roundhay 1p *West Yorkshire Archive Service, Leeds*

33808 Leeds: Headingley St Columba United Reformed Church 10pp *West Yorkshire Archive Service, Leeds*

33809 Rawdon Congregational Church 3pp *West Yorkshire Archive Service, Leeds*

33810 Leeds: Mill Hill Unitarian Church 2pp *West Yorkshire Archive Service, Leeds*

33811 Leeds and district Baptist marriage registers 2pp *West Yorkshire Archive Service, Leeds*

33812 Leeds: Killingbeck Roman Catholic Cemetery 2pp *Private*

33813 Thomas and William Oakes Hunt, solicitors, Stratford-on-Avon 87pp *Shakespeare Birthplace Trust Records Office*

33814 Leeds: Mount St Mary Roman Catholic Church, Richmond Hill 2pp *Private*

33815 Leeds: Sacred Heart Roman Catholic Church, Burley 3pp *Private*

33816 Leeds: Our Lady of Good Counsel Roman Catholic Church, Horsforth 5pp *Private*

33817 Scottish trade associations 7pp *Glasgow University Archives and Business Record Centre*

33818 City of Leeds Young Mens Christian Association 8pp *West Yorkshire Archive Service, Leeds*

33819 Leeds: St James's University Hospital 6pp *West Yorkshire Archive Service, Leeds*

33820 National Trust for Scotland: Scotland's Gardens Scheme 5pp *Private*

33821 Leeds: Kirkstall Ward Conservative Association 2pp *West Yorkshire Archive Service, Leeds*

33822 Wetherby & District Conservative Club Ltd 4pp *West Yorkshire Archive Service, Leeds*

33823 Leeds Trade Union and Community Resource and Information Centre 3pp *West Yorkshire Archive Service, Leeds*

33824 Leeds Chest and Heart Association 2pp *West Yorkshire Archive Service, Leeds*

33825 Leeds Fireclay Co Ltd 2pp *West Yorkshire Archive Service, Leeds*

33826 George William Black, ophthalmic surgeon: professional and personal papers 3pp *West Yorkshire Archive Service, Leeds*

33827 Leeds: East Moor Community Home School 9pp *West Yorkshire Archive Service, Leeds*

33828 Leeds: St Patricks Roman Catholic Church, New York Road 5pp *Private*

33829 Robert Sunter, bookseller, York: corresp 3pp *West Yorkshire Archive Service, Leeds*

33830 John Keble, cleric and poet: corresp 18pp *Hampshire Record Office*

33831 Free Church of Scotland Colonial, Continental and Jewish Mission Committee 4pp *National Library of Scotland, Department of Manuscripts*

33832 Leeds: Woodhouse Lane Methodist New Connexion Chapel 2pp *West Yorkshire Archive Service, Leeds*

33833 C & J Smithson Ltd, worsted mfrs, Halifax incl Park Print Works Ltd 4pp *West Yorkshire Archive Service, Calderdale*

33834 Sir Arthur Schuster, physicist: corresp and papers 19pp *Manchester University: John Rylands Library*

33835 Robert Salmon Hutton, metallurgist: corresp and papers 12pp *Manchester University: John Rylands Library*

33836 Sir Henry Enfield Roscoe, chemist: corresp and papers 6pp *Manchester University: John Rylands Library*

*33837 Sir William Boyd Dawkins, geologist: corresp and papers 26pp *Manchester University: John Rylands Library*

33838 H Wagstaff & Son, watchmakers and jewellers, Leek 1p *Staffordshire Record Office*

33839 George Salter & Co Ltd, spring balance mfrs, West Bromwich 47pp *Staffordshire Record Office*

33840 Darlington Constituency Labour Party 2pp *Durham County Record Office*

33841 Darlington Town Mission 3pp *Durham County Record Office*

33842 John Pease, Quaker minister: diaries 11pp *Durham County Record Office*

33843 Fleming family, land agents, Tudhoe 50pp *Durham County Record Office*

33844 Teesdale and Wear Valley Petty Sessions 3pp *Durham County Record Office*

33845 Association of Teachers in Technical Institutions: North Midlands division 3pp *Derbyshire Record Office*

33846 Chesterfield and District Society for the Deaf 1p *Derbyshire Record Office*

33847 Melbourne Rural Deanery 1p *Derbyshire Record Office*

33848 Longford Rural Deanery 1p
Derbyshire Record Office
33849 Wirksworth Rural Deanery 1p
Derbyshire Record Office
33850 Ashbourne Gas Co Ltd 2pp
Derbyshire Record Office
33851 Hawkesbury Rural Deanery 1p
Gloucestershire Record Office
33852 Belper: Babington Hospital
12pp *Derbyshire Record Office*
33853 House of Andrews Ltd,
stationers and booksellers,
Durham 19pp *Durham County
Record Office*
33854 Clapham United Reformed
Church 13pp *Greater London
Record Office and History Library*
33855 Major-General Reginald Henry
Whitworth: letters and papers
9pp *Imperial War Museum
Department of Documents*
33856 Dame Naomi Margaret
Mitchison, writer: corresp 6pp
*Imperial War Museum
Department of Documents*
33857 Admiral Sir Gerald Charles
Dickens: diaries, corresp and
papers 4pp *Imperial War Museum
Department of Documents*
33858 William Thomas Swift, school-
master: diaries and notebooks
91pp *Gloucestershire Record Office*
33859 Ward & Woodman, chemists,
Gloucester 4pp *Gloucestershire
Record Office*
33860 London: Elizabeth Garrett
Anderson Hospital 19pp
*Greater London Record Office
and History Library*
33861 National Union of Agricultural
Workers: Gloucestershire County
Committee and district
committees 3pp *Gloucestershire
Record Office*
33862 Gloucester Civic Trust 20pp
Gloucestershire Record Office
33863 Ancient Society of Crypt
Youths 1p *Gloucestershire
Record Office*
*33864 Sir Graham Selby Wilson,
microbiologist: corresp and
papers 66pp *Wellcome Institute
for the History of Medicine*
33865 Helen Waddell, historian:
corresp and papers 81pp
*Queens University of Belfast
Library*
33866 Thomas Andrews, chemist:
corresp and papers 7pp *Queens
University of Belfast Library*

33867 Fakenham and Wells
Methodist Circuit 5pp *Norfolk
Record Office*
33868 South Lopham Townlands
Charity 9pp *Norfolk Record
Office*
33869 Alburgh Town Lands Estate
Charity 4pp *Norfolk Record
Office*
33870 Stimpson family, farmers,
Great Witchingham 2pp
Norfolk Record Office
33871 East Dereham Urban District
Council 13pp *Norfolk Record
Office*
33872 John Colin Campbell Davidson,
1st Viscount Davidson: corresp
and papers[1] 103pp *House of
Lords Record Office*
33873 National Union of Teachers:
North East Cheshire Teachers
Association 2pp *Cheshire
Record Office*
33874 James Hall, local historian:
notebooks 3pp *Cheshire Record
Office*
33875 Cuninghame family of
Caprington: deeds and papers
incl royal letter books 81pp
Scottish Record Office
33876 Ilford South Labour Party:
Central Womens Section 2pp
*Greater London Record Office
and History Library*
33877 Charity Commission: Cheshire
charities accounts 34pp
Cheshire Record Office
33878 Knutsford: Brook Street
Unitarian Chapel and
Allostock Unitarian Chapel
7pp *Cheshire Record Office*
33879 Alexander, Fergusson & Co
Ltd, lead and paint mfrs,
Glasgow 6pp *Glasgow
University Archives and Business
Record Centre*
33880 Tonbridge Methodist Circuit
12pp *Centre for Kentish Studies*
33881 Tunbridge Wells Methodist
Circuit 13pp *Centre for Kentish
Studies*
33882 Cheshire Insurance Committee
2pp *Cheshire Record Office*
33883 Cuninghame family of
Craigends: deeds and estate
papers 59pp *Scottish Record
Office*

---

[1]*Descriptive List of the Papers of John Colin Campbell
Davidson, MP, First Viscount Davidson, 1990*

33884 Faithful Thomas, lawyer and coroner: calendars of Chester Palatinate records 5pp *Cheshire Record Office*

33885 Eadie Bros & Co Ltd, ring and ring traveller mfrs, Paisley 10pp *Paisley Museum, Art Gallery and Coats Observatory*

33886 Burtonwood: St Paul of the Cross Roman Catholic parish 1p *Cheshire Record Office*

33887 AF Craig & Co Ltd, engineers and ironfounders, Paisley 5pp *Paisley Museum, Art Gallery and Coats Observatory*

33888 Robertson family of Kindeace: family and estate papers 19pp *Scottish Record Office*

33889 Christian Brotherly Society 9pp *Greater London Record Office and History Library*

33890 Crewe: Hill Street Presbyterian Church of England 1p *Cheshire Record Office*

33891 Northwich: Victoria Infirmary 2pp *Cheshire Record Office*

33892 Cheshire Area Health Authority 5pp *Cheshire Record Office*

33893 Winsford: Albert Infirmary 1p *Cheshire Record Office*

33894 Weaverham: The Grange Hospital 1p *Cheshire Record Office*

33895 Coventry Victor Motor Co Ltd, diesel engine mfrs 4pp *Coventry City Record Office*

*33896 William Horsley, composer: personal and family corresp and papers 74pp *Oxford University: Bodleian Library, Department of Western Manuscripts*

33897 Brudenell-Bruce family, Marquesses of Ailesbury: family and Yorkshire estate papers 560pp *North Yorkshire County Record Office*

33898 William Smith, politician: personal and family corresp and papers 13pp *Cambridge University Library, Department of Manuscripts and University Archives*

33899 Grand United Order of Oddfellows: Halton and Runcorn District Lodge 628 2pp *Cheshire Record Office*

33900 Campbell family, baronets, of Barcaldine: family and estate papers 678pp *Scottish Record Office*

33901 Christopher Egleton of Ellesborough: Buckinghamshire manor records 10pp *Buckinghamshire Record Office*

33902 Hamilton Bruce family of Falkland: family and estate papers 40pp *Scottish Record Office*

33903 Agnew family, baronets, of Lochnaw: family and estate papers 127pp *Scottish Record Office*

33904 Ross family of Cromarty: deeds and papers 7pp *Scottish Record Office*

33905 Burnett family of Barns: family and estate papers 6pp *Scottish Record Office*

33906 Werrington estate 146pp *Cornwall Record Office*

33907 High Wycombe and District War Memorial Hospital 1p *Buckinghamshire Record Office*

33908 Chesham Labour Party and Chesham Trades Council 1p *Buckinghamshire Record Office*

33909 Prestwood Horse Show and Agricultural Society 2pp *Buckinghamshire Record Office*

33910 Aylesbury Town Cricket Club 2pp *Buckinghamshire Record Office*

33911 Jones family of Stoneleigh and Leamington Spa, solicitors: papers 4pp *Shakespeare Birthplace Trust Records Office*

33912 Merton Borough 3pp *Surrey Record Office*

33913 Royal Surrey School of Nursing Appeals 4pp *Surrey Record Office*

33914 National Council on Inland Transport 91pp *Doncaster Archives Department*

33915 Rowlands family of Plastirion: family and estate papers 17pp *Gwynedd Archives and Museums Service, Caernarfon Area Record Office*

33916 Babcock International plc, mechanical engineers, London 300pp *Glasgow University Archives and Business Record Centre*

33917 Hughes family of Cefn Mawr: deeds and papers incl Owen family of Plas Penrhyn and Rhuddgaer 223pp *Gwynedd Archives and Museums Service, Llangefni Area Record Office*

33918 Labour Party Wales 42pp *National Library of Wales, Department of Manuscripts and Records*

33919 Lloyd family of Tynewydd, Llannor: deeds and papers 210pp *Gwynedd Archives and Museums Service, Caernarfon Area Record Office*

33920 Plymouth: St Budeaux School Foundation Charity 9pp *West Devon Area Record Office*

33921 Natural History Museum: Trustees and Directorate papers 44pp *Natural History Museum*

33922 Farley's Infant Food Ltd, Plymouth 4pp *West Devon Area Record Office*

33923 Culme-Seymour family, baronets, of Rockingham Castle, Northamptonshire: deeds and papers rel to Plymouth estate 36pp *West Devon Area Record Office*

33924 Tavistock: Maynard's Charity and Ford Street almshouses 5pp *West Devon Area Record Office*

33925 Devonport: Keyham Methodist Church 1p *West Devon Area Record Office*

33926 ANL Munby, librarian and bibliographer: corresp with JW Carter 5pp *Cambridge University: Kings College Modern Records Centre*

33927 Buckingham family: corresp with EM Forster 14pp *Cambridge University: Kings College Modern Records Centre*

33928 William Charles Green, classical scholar: misc corresp and papers 3pp *Cambridge University: Kings College Modern Records Centre*

33929 John Reginald Lang-Hyde, author: literary papers 3pp *Cambridge University: Kings College Modern Records Centre*

33930 Cambridge University: King's College Library Modern Archive Centre misc accessions 4pp *Cambridge University: Kings College Modern Records Centre*

33931 Sir George Walter Prothero, historian: journals and notebooks 4pp *Cambridge University: Kings College Modern Records Centre*

33932 Dyfed County Council 12pp *Dyfed Archives Service, Carmarthenshire Area Record Office*

33933 Bright family of Totterton: family and estate papers 155pp *Shropshire Records and Research Unit*

33934 Cardigan Rural District Council 7pp *Dyfed Archives Service, Cardiganshire Area Record Office*

33935 Welsh Water Authority, Cardiganshire: records of predecessor bodies 52pp *Dyfed Archives Service, Cardiganshire Area Record Office*

33936 Cardiganshire registers of duties on land values 10pp *Dyfed Archives Service, Cardiganshire Area Record Office*

33937 Aberystwyth shipping registers 1p *Dyfed Archives Service, Cardiganshire Area Record Office*

33938 Cooper & Co, solicitors, Much Wenlock: clients papers 113pp *Shropshire Records and Research Unit*

33939 Middlewich Petty Sessions 2pp *Cheshire Record Office*

33940 Sandbach Petty Sessions 2pp *Cheshire Record Office*

33941 Congleton Petty Sessions 5pp *Cheshire Record Office*

33942 Congleton Borough Petty Sessions 3pp *Cheshire Record Office*

33943 Mid-Cheshire Post Office and Telecommunications Advisory Committee 1p *Cheshire Record Office*

33944 Poynton Miners Association 1p *Cheshire Record Office*

33945 Maryon-Wilson family, baronets, of East Borne, Sussex: Charlton estate papers 272pp *Greater London Record Office and History Library*

33946 Scott family of Betton: family and estate papers 249pp *Shropshire Records and Research Unit*

33947 Royal British Legion: Berrington branch 1p *Shropshire Records and Research Unit*

33948 Shropshire Chamber of Agriculture 1p *Shropshire Records and Research Unit*

33949 Wace, Morgan & Co, solicitors, Shrewsbury: deeds and papers 198pp *Shropshire Records and Research Unit*

33950 Hanmer family of Pentrepant: family and estate papers 250pp *Shropshire Records and Research Unit*

33951 Cotes family of Woodcote: estate papers 7pp *Shropshire Records and Research Unit*

33952 Oxford University: Regents Park College: misc accessions 14pp *Oxford University: Regents Park College, Angus Library*

33953 International Order of Good Templars: Grimsby and Little Coates 3pp *South Humberside Area Archive Office*

33954 Scunthorpe and District Working Mens Club 4pp *South Humberside Area Archive Office*

33955 Grimsby: Freeman Street General Baptist Church 1p *South Humberside Area Archive Office*

33956 Kinchant family of Park Hall: deeds and papers 48pp *Shropshire Records and Research Unit*

33957 Pritchard family, solicitors and bankers, Broseley: clients papers 31pp *Shropshire Records and Research Unit*

33958 Sydney Raine: Shropshire local history collection 50pp *Shropshire Records and Research Unit*

33959 Copley family, baronets, of Sprotbrough: family and estate papers 8pp *West Yorkshire Archive Service, Yorkshire Archaeological Society*

33960 Wentworth family, Earls of Strafford: misc estate papers 13pp *West Yorkshire Archive Service, Yorkshire Archaeological Society*

33961 Wombwell family, baronets, of Newburgh Priory: papers, incl family and estate papers of the Belasyse family, Viscounts Fauconberg 36pp *North Yorkshire County Record Office*

33962 Warrington Borough Petty Sessions 10pp *Cheshire Record Office*

33963 Hatt Cook Chambers & Kershaw, solicitors, Northwich: Cheshire election papers 4pp *Cheshire Record Office*

33964 Islington: Elizabeth Fry Probation Hostel 4pp *Hackney Archives Department*

33965 Kilvert Society 6pp *Hereford Record Office*

33966 Hereford County College 2pp *Hereford Record Office*

33967 South Hackney: Trinity Congregational Church 2pp *Hackney Archives Department*

33968 Money-Kyrle family of Whetham House, Wiltshire (formerly of Homme House, Herefordshire): corresp and papers 13pp *Hereford Record Office*

33969 Womens National Cancer Control Campaign: Hackney and district branch 1p *Hackney Archives Department*

33970 South Herefordshire District Council 1p *Hereford Record Office*

33971 De Beauvoir Association 2pp *Hackney Archives Department*

33972 Robinson's Retreat and Robinson's Relief Fund 2pp *Hackney Archives Department*

33973 Royal Welsh Yacht Club, Caernarfon 28pp *Gwynedd Archives and Museums Service, Caernarfon Area Record Office*

33974 Golden Valley Railway Co 4pp *Hereford Record Office*

33975 Hughes family of Ty Mawr Mynydd, Holyhead: family corresp 30pp *Gwynedd Archives and Museums Service, Llangefni Area Record Office*

33976 John Lloyd Jones: papers rel to the Welsh Chapel, Talbot Street, Dublin 8pp *Gwynedd Archives and Museums Service, Llangefni Area Record Office*

33977 George Russell & Co Ltd, engineers and crane mfrs, Motherwell 1p *Strathclyde Regional Archives*

33978 David Carlaw (Engineers) Ltd, envelope machine mfrs, Glasgow 1p *Strathclyde Regional Archives*

33979 Andrews & Cameron Ltd, engineers, valve and evaporating machinery mfrs, Kirkintilloch 1p *Strathclyde Regional Archives*

33980 Coltness Iron Co Ltd, coal and iron masters, Newmains 3pp *Strathclyde Regional Archives*

33981 South Pembrokeshire District Council 11pp *Dyfed Archives Service, Pembrokeshire Area Record Office*

33982 Robert HG Smallwood, antiquarian: MS collections 300pp *National Library of Wales, Department of Manuscripts and Records*

33983 Edward Thomas John, industrialist and politician: corresp and papers 1219pp *National Library of Wales, Department of Manuscripts and Records*

33984 Ruthin Lordship: deeds and papers 566pp *National Library of Wales, Department of Manuscripts and Records*

33985 Saunders, Shepherd & Co Ltd, manufacturing jewellers and goldsmiths, London 10pp *Private*

33986 Melyn Tinplate Co Ltd, tinplate mfrs, Neath 1p *Glamorgan Record Office*

33987 John Freeman & Copper Co, copper mfrs, Llansamlet 6pp *Glamorgan Record Office*

33988 Sheppard & Sons Ltd, conveyor mfrs and structural engineers, Bridgend 10pp *Glamorgan Record Office*

33989 Melingriffith Co Ltd, tinplate mfrs, Cardiff 4pp *Glamorgan Record Office*

33990 Lewis family, farmers, Potterslade Farm, Llawhaden 5pp *Dyfed Archives Service, Pembrokeshire Area Record Office*

33991 Solva Memorial Hall Committee 1p *Dyfed Archives Service, Pembrokeshire Area Record Office*

33992 Skone family, farmers, Hodgeston 1p *Dyfed Archives Service, Pembrokeshire Area Record Office*

33993 Thomas Lawrence, smith, Wiston 1p *Dyfed Archives Service, Pembrokeshire Area Record Office*

33994 Narberth Joint Burial Board 1p *Dyfed Archives Service, Pembrokeshire Area Record Office*

33995 Sydney G Phillips, outfitter, Haverfordwest 1p *Dyfed Archives Service, Pembrokeshire Area Record Office*

33996 Barker Ellis Silver Co Ltd, silversmiths and electroplaters, Birmingham 9pp *Private*

33997 Whitley Bay: St Margaret's Methodist Church 1p *Tyne and Wear Archives Service*

33998 Murton: Church Street Methodist Church 1p *Tyne and Wear Archives Service*

33999 Murton: Greenhill Methodist Church 1p *Tyne and Wear Archives Service*

*34000 John Frank Adams, mathematician: corresp and papers 120pp *Cambridge University: Trinity College Library*

34001 Murton Methodist Church 1p *Tyne and Wear Archives Service*

34002 Murton Colliery Methodist Church 1p *Tyne and Wear Archives Service*

34003 Murton Colliery Wesley Methodist Church 1p *Tyne and Wear Archives Service*

34004 Easington Lane: Central Methodist Church 1p *Tyne and Wear Archives Service*

34005 South Hetton: Richmond Street Methodist Church 1p *Tyne and Wear Archives Service*

34006 Moorsley Wesley Methodist Church 1p *Tyne and Wear Archives Service*

34007 Pembrokeshire womens institutes 10pp *Dyfed Archives Service, Pembrokeshire Area Record Office*

34008 National and Local Government Officers Association: Pembrokeshire branch 5pp *Dyfed Archives Service, Pembrokeshire Area Record Office*

34009 National Farmers Union: Pembrokeshire county branch 75pp *Dyfed Archives Service, Pembrokeshire Area Record Office*

34010 C Hole, grocer and provision factor, Milford Haven 1p *Dyfed Archives Service, Pembrokeshire Area Record Office*

34011 Milford Haven Urban District Council 61pp *Dyfed Archives Service, Pembrokeshire Area Record Office*

34012 Cemaes Rural District Council 8pp *Dyfed Archives Service, Pembrokeshire Area Record Office*

34013 Cardigan Mercantile Co Ltd, builders' merchants 4pp *Dyfed Archives Service, Pembrokeshire Area Record Office*

34014 Independent Order of Rechabites: Pembrokeshire district 2pp *Dyfed Archives Service, Pembrokeshire Area Record Office*

34015 A & R Wehrle, pawnbrokers, Llanelli 1p *Dyfed Archives Service, Carmarthenshire Area Record Office*

34016 Milford Haven Dock & Railway Co 8pp *Dyfed Archives Service, Pembrokeshire Area Record Office*

34017 William Bennett, draper and general dealer, Dinas 5pp *Dyfed Archives Service, Pembrokeshire Area Record Office*

34018 WG & JA Harries, chemists, Haverfordwest 2pp *Dyfed Archives Service, Pembrokeshire Area Record Office*

34019 Friends of the Pembrokeshire Museum 2pp *Dyfed Archives Service, Pembrokeshire Area Record Office*

34020 Thomas Tamlyn, surveyor, Haverfordwest 11pp *Dyfed Archives Service, Pembrokeshire Area Record Office*

34021 Pembrokeshire County Nursing Association 2pp *Dyfed Archives Service, Pembrokeshire Area Record Office*

34022 Haverfordwest Rotary Club 1p *Dyfed Archives Service, Pembrokeshire Area Record Office*

34023 Haverfordwest Arts Club 5pp *Dyfed Archives Service, Pembrokeshire Area Record Office*

34024 Pembroke Dock Harlequins Rugby Club 2pp *Dyfed Archives Service, Pembrokeshire Area Record Office*

34025 Pembrokeshire County Club 3pp *Dyfed Archives Service, Pembrokeshire Area Record Office*

34026 Neyland Rugby Club 1p *Dyfed Archives Service, Pembrokeshire Area Record Office*

34027 Milford Haven Sailors Rest 2pp *Dyfed Archives Service, Pembrokeshire Area Record Office*

34028 Pembrokeshire Record Society 1p *Dyfed Archives Service, Pembrokeshire Area Record Office*

34029 Saundersfoot: Evelyn Coffee Tavern 1p *Dyfed Archives Service, Pembrokeshire Area Record Office*

34030 Pembrokeshire County Badminton Association 2pp *Dyfed Archives Service, Pembrokeshire Area Record Office*

34031 Haverfordwest Inner Wheel Club 2pp *Dyfed Archives Service, Pembrokeshire Area Record Office*

34032 Joseph William Hammond & Co Ltd, stationers, printers and publishers, Haverfordwest 4pp *Dyfed Archives Service, Pembrokeshire Area Record Office*

34033 Electrical Association for Women: Haverfordwest branch 2pp *Dyfed Archives Service, Pembrokeshire Area Record Office*

34034 Sealyham Terrier Club 4pp *Dyfed Archives Service, Pembrokeshire Area Record Office*

34035 Seven Day Opening Campaign 1p *Dyfed Archives Service, Carmarthenshire Area Record Office*

34036 Council for the Protection of Rural Wales: Pembrokeshire branch 2pp *Dyfed Archives Service, Pembrokeshire Area Record Office*

34037 Pembrokeshire Local History Society 2pp *Dyfed Archives Service, Pembrokeshire Area Record Office*

34038 North Devon Film Society 1p *North Devon Record Office*

34039 RTP Williams & Sons, solicitors: Milford Haven office 543pp *Dyfed Archives Service, Pembrokeshire Area Record Office*

34040 Haverfordwest Temperance Hall Trust 7pp *Dyfed Archives Service, Pembrokeshire Area Record Office*

34041 Haverfordwest: James Griffith's Charity 2pp *Dyfed Archives Service, Pembrokeshire Area Record Office*

34042 Eaton-Evans & Morris, solicitors, Haverfordwest: clients papers 216pp *Dyfed Archives Service, Pembrokeshire Area Record Office*

34043 Neyland Labour Party 1p *Dyfed Archives Service, Pembrokeshire Area Record Office*

34044 Ancient Order of Foresters: Elland and Ripponden district 5pp *West Yorkshire Archive Service, Calderdale*

34045 Haverfordwest Bridge Commissioners 14pp *Dyfed Archives Service, Pembrokeshire Area Record Office*

34046 Haverfordwest: St Martin's Joint Burial Board 6pp *Dyfed Archives Service, Pembrokeshire Area Record Office*

34047 Barnard Castle Rural Deanery 2pp *Durham County Record Office*

34048 Joseph Wright & Co Ltd, chain mfrs, Tipton 9pp *Sandwell District Libraries*

34049 Winchester: St Pauls Hospital 2pp *Hampshire Record Office*

34050 Ringwood Electric Supply Co Ltd 5pp *Hampshire Record Office*

34051 Milford Port Health Authority 5pp *Dyfed Archives Service, Pembrokeshire Area Record Office*

34052 Tasker-Evans family of Upton Castle: corresp and papers 40pp *Dyfed Archives Service, Pembrokeshire Area Record Office*

*34053 Nevill Henry Kendal Aylmer Coghill, literary scholar: corresp and papers 40pp *Oxford University: Bodleian Library, Department of Western Manuscripts*

34054 John Bowling & Co Ltd, ironfounders, Leeds 1p *Leeds University, Brotherton Library*

34055 William David Phillips, auctioneer, estate agent and landlord of the Salutation Hotel, Haverfordwest: corresp and papers 11pp *Dyfed Archives Service, Pembrokeshire Area Record Office*

34056 Pembrokeshire County Museum: MS collection 14pp *Dyfed Archives Service, Pembrokeshire Area Record Office*

34057 Cornercroft Ltd, motor vehicle and aircraft component mfrs, Coventry 7pp *Coventry City Record Office*

34058 Dibb Lupton & Co, solicitors, Leeds 200pp *West Yorkshire Archive Service, Leeds*

34059 Henderson family of Fordell: family and estate papers 420pp *Scottish Record Office*

34060 Shaw, Mottershead & Badgery, solicitors, Colne 119pp *West Yorkshire Archive Service, Leeds*

34061 Maclaine family of Lochbuie: family and estate papers 233pp *Scottish Record Office*

*34062 John Davy Hayward, anthologist and bibliophile: corresp and papers 16pp *Cambridge University: Kings College Modern Records Centre*

34063 Louis Mountbatten, Earl Mountbatten of Burma: corresp and papers[1] 309pp *Southampton University Library*

34064 WH Roscoe Howells, author, journalist and farmer: literary MSS, corresp and papers 11pp *Dyfed Archives Service, Pembrokeshire Area Record Office*

34065 Samuel Birkett Ltd, brass founders and valve mfrs, Cleckheaton and Heckmondwike 2pp *West Yorkshire Archive Service, Kirklees*

34066 Richard Carter Ltd, shovel mfrs, Kirkburton 2pp *West Yorkshire Archive Service, Kirklees*

---

[1]LM Mitchell, KJ Sampson and CM Woolgar (eds): *A Summary Catalogue of the Papers of Earl Mountbatten of Burma*, 1991

34067 Haigh-Chadwick Ltd, textile machinery mfrs, Huddersfield 15pp *West Yorkshire Archive Service, Kirklees*

34068 Hanson Dale & Co Ltd, lead mfrs, Huddersfield 9pp *West Yorkshire Archive Service, Kirklees*

34069 A Hirst & Son Ltd, electrical engineers, Dewsbury 3pp *West Yorkshire Archive Service, Kirklees*

34070 Joseph Kilner & Son, heald and slay mfrs, Honley 4pp *West Yorkshire Archive Service, Kirklees*

34071 Rippon Brothers Ltd, coachbuilders, Huddersfield 1p *West Yorkshire Archive Service, Kirklees*

34072 Hull and Goole Port Sanitary Authority 29pp *Kingston upon Hull City Record Office*

34073 Williams & Williams, solicitors, Fishguard 18pp *Dyfed Archives Service, Pembrokeshire Area Record Office*

34074 Josiah Fairbank & Son, surveyors, Sheffield 12pp *Sheffield Archives*

34075 Beale family of Standen: papers 15pp *West Sussex Record Office*

34076 Lowless & Lowless, solicitors, Pembroke and Pembroke Dock 322pp *Dyfed Archives Service, Pembrokeshire Area Record Office*

34077 Ely: Countess of Huntingdon's Chapel 6pp *Private*

34078 Davies Bryan family of Caernarfon: corresp and papers 45pp *Gwynedd Archives and Museums Service, Caernarfon Area Record Office*

34079 Allen family of Cresselly: deeds and papers 25pp *Dyfed Archives Service, Pembrokeshire Area Record Office*

34080 Lewis & James, solicitors, Narberth 268pp *Dyfed Archives Service, Pembrokeshire Area Record Office*

34081 Wyndham-Quin family, Earls of Dunraven and Mountearl: manorial records and estate papers 10pp *National Library of Wales, Department of Manuscripts and Records*

34082 Davies Brothers, slate merchants, Porthmadog 15pp *Gwynedd Archives and Museums Service, Caernarfon Area Record Office*

34083 Cathcart family of Genoch and Knockdolian: family and estate papers 99pp *Scottish Record Office*

34084 N Downing & Sons Ltd, ironfounders, Stockton-on-Tees 1p *Cleveland Archives Section*

34085 Harker & Sons (Engineers) Ltd, general engineers and precision machinists, Stockton-on-Tees 1p *Cleveland Archives Section*

34086 Thomas Allan & Sons Ltd, ironfounders, Thornaby-on-Tees 3pp *Cleveland Archives Section*

34087 W Richards & Sons Ltd, ironfounders, Middlesbrough 2pp *Cleveland Archives Section*

34088 Planet magazine 8pp *National Library of Wales, Department of Manuscripts and Records*

34089 Mostyn-Owen family of Woodhouse: deeds and papers 117pp *Shropshire Records and Research Unit*

34090 Ross family of Pitcalnie: family and estate papers 47pp *Scottish Record Office*

34091 Salwey & Rickards, solicitors, Ludlow 156pp *Shropshire Records and Research Unit*

34092 Leith-Ross family of Arnage: family and estate papers 5pp *Aberdeen University Library, Dept of Special Collections and Archives*

34093 Haldane family of Gleneagles, Perthshire: deeds 58pp *Scottish Record Office*

34094 Lloyd-Jones family of Kilsall and Shackerley: family and estate papers 148pp *Shropshire Records and Research Unit*

34095 Smythe family of Methven: family and estate papers 33pp *Scottish Record Office*

34096 Philip Maynard Williams, historian and political scientist: corresp and papers 24pp *Oxford University: Nuffield College Library*

34097 Warner & Co Ltd, refined pig iron mfrs, Middlesbrough 8pp *Cleveland Archives Section*

34098 Head Wrightson & Co Ltd, engineers, Thornaby-on-Tees 41pp *Cleveland Archives Section*

34099 Ramsay-Steel-Maitland family, baronets, of Sauchie: family and estate papers 147pp *Scottish Record Office*

34100 Stewart family of Massater: deeds and estate papers 44pp *Scottish Record Office*

34101 Graham-Stirling family of Strowan: deeds and estate papers 15pp *Scottish Record Office*

34102 Cochrane (Middlesbrough) Foundry Ltd, ironfounders and cast iron pipe mfrs 3pp *Cleveland Archives Section*

34103 Aberdeen Chamber of Commerce 13pp *Aberdeen City Archives*

34104 Wilson & Longbottom Ltd, loom makers, Barnsley 1p *Barnsley Archive Service*

34105 J & G Grant, whisky distillers, Ballindalloch 11pp *Private*

34106 Bayerisches Hauptstaatsarchiv: MS collections relating to Scotland 11pp *Bayerisches Hauptstaatsarchiv*

34107 Cannon Industries Ltd, mfrs of domestic gas and electrical appliances and chemical plant equipment, Coseley 16pp *Private*

34108 Peden & Patrick, solicitors, Glasgow 6pp *Strathclyde Regional Archives*

34109 Dundee Society for Prevention of Cruelty to Children 6pp *Dundee District Archive and Record Centre*

34110 Wellwood/Leslie, architects, Dundee 22pp *Dundee District Archive and Record Centre*

34111 William Henry Mainwaring MP: corresp and papers 4pp *National Library of Wales, Department of Manuscripts and Records*

34112 Robin Page Arnot, communist writer and historian: corresp and papers 38pp *Hull University, Brynmor Jones Library*

34113 Scottish Universities Physical Education Association 4pp *Glasgow University Archives and Business Record Centre*

34114 Scottish University Management Services and Efficiency Unit 15pp *Glasgow University Archives and Business Record Centre*

34115 Johnstone family of Alva: family and estate papers 25pp *Private*

34116 Frederick William Dalley, trade unionist: corresp and papers 11pp *Hull University, Brynmor Jones Library*

34117 Philip Arthur Larkin, poet: corresp and papers 22pp *Hull University, Brynmor Jones Library*

34118 Hull University Library: friendly society records 26pp *Hull University, Brynmor Jones Library*

34119 Maclean family of Kinloch and Drimnin: corresp and papers 19pp *Private*

34120 Harold Jones: corresp rel to a proposed Trades Union Congress for Wales 147pp *National Library of Wales, Department of Manuscripts and Records*

34121 Diss Citizens Advice Bureau 2pp *Norfolk Record Office*

34122 Long & Beck, auctioneers and estate agents, Fakenham 3pp *Norfolk Record Office*

34123 Maurice M Schofield, historian: shipping research papers 19pp *Liverpool University Archives Unit*

34124 Mawson, Swan & Morgan Ltd, booksellers and stationers, Newcastle upon Tyne 17pp *Tyne and Wear Archives Service*

34125 Daniel Doncaster & Sons Ltd, steel converters, Sheffield 5pp *Kelham Island Industrial Museum*

34126 WJ Price & Co Ltd and GW Millichap & Partners, auctioneers, estate agents and surveyors, Brecon 44pp *Powys County Archives Office*

34127 Jarrow Borough 1p *Tyne and Wear Archives Service*

34128 Yorkshire Water Authority: Western Division 12pp *West Yorkshire Archive Service, Calderdale*

34129 Hepton Rural District Council 23pp *West Yorkshire Archive Service, Calderdale*

34130 Bromley-by-Bow: St Andrew's Hospital 12pp *Royal London Hospital Archives Centre and Museum*

34131 Gateshead Family Practitioner Committee 5pp *Tyne and Wear Archives Service*

34132 Alfred Owen Williams, poet and author: corresp and literary MSS 5pp *Wiltshire Record Office*

34133 Chippenham Borough 1p *Wiltshire Record Office*

34134 Swindon Chamber of Commerce 2pp *Wiltshire Record Office*

34135 Wiltshire Music Festival 2pp *Wiltshire Record Office*

34136 Dilton Nursing Association 1p *Wiltshire Record Office*

34137 Cherhill Womens Institute 1p *Wiltshire Record Office*

34138 Fovant and Sutton Mandeville Womens Institute 1p *Wiltshire Record Office*

34139 Yarnbury Womens Institute 1p *Wiltshire Record Office*

34140 National and Local Government Officers Association: Wiltshire branch 2pp *Wiltshire Record Office*

34141 Bristol Association of Church Bell Ringers: Swindon branch 1p *Wiltshire Record Office*

34142 Seend Womens Institute 3pp *Wiltshire Record Office*

34143 Salisbury Conservative Association 2pp *Wiltshire Record Office*

34144 Education Welfare Officers National Association: Wiltshire branch 1p *Wiltshire Record Office*

34145 Sunderland: Grindon Methodist Church 1p *Tyne and Wear Archives Service*

34146 Sunderland: Dove Street Methodist Church, Pallion 1p *Tyne and Wear Archives Service*

34147 Sunderland Fourth Primitive Methodist Circuit 1p *Tyne and Wear Archives Service*

34148 Ryhope: Cliff Road Methodist Church 1p *Tyne and Wear Archives Service*

34149 Sunderland: Park Road Methodist Church 1p *Tyne and Wear Archives Service*

34150 Sunderland: Pallion Road Methodist Church 1p *Tyne and Wear Archives Service*

34151 Rotherham & Sons Ltd, precision engineers and watch mfrs, Coventry 13pp *Coventry City Record Office*

34152 Sunderland: Tatham Street Methodist Church 1p *Tyne and Wear Archives Service*

34153 Sunderland: Grangetown Memorial Wesleyan Church 1p *Tyne and Wear Archives Service*

34154 Sunderland: George Street Methodist Church, Deptford 1p *Tyne and Wear Archives Service*

34155 Sunderland: Carol Street Methodist Church 1p *Tyne and Wear Archives Service*

34156 Sunderland: Ballast Hills Wesleyan Methodist Church 1p *Tyne and Wear Archives Service*

34157 Sunderland: High Street East Methodist Mission 1p *Tyne and Wear Archives Service*

34158 South Shields: Whiteleas Methodist Church 1p *Tyne and Wear Archives Service*

34159 South Hetton Methodist Church 1p *Tyne and Wear Archives Service*

34160 Hetton-le-Hole: Union Street Methodist Church 1p *Tyne and Wear Archives Service*

34161 Hetton-le-Hole: Front Street Methodist Church 3pp *Tyne and Wear Archives Service*

34162 Hetton Downs: Chapel Street Methodist Church 1p *Tyne and Wear Archives Service*

34163 Hetton Downs: High Downs Methodist Church 2pp *Tyne and Wear Archives Service*

34164 Easington Lane Wesley Methodist Chapel 1p *Tyne and Wear Archives Service*

34165 Hestair Dennis Ltd, commercial vehicle mfrs, Guildford 75pp *Surrey Record Office, Guildford Muniment Room*

34166 Workers Educational Association: Guildford district 3pp *Surrey Record Office, Guildford Muniment Room*

34167 Joseph Lloyd & Co, solicitors, Rhyl: clients papers 243pp *Clwyd Record Office, Hawarden Branch*

34168 Thomas Coke, methodist preacher and missionary: corresp and papers 137pp *Manchester University: Methodist Archives and Research Centre*

34169 John Merewether, physician, Market Lavington: diaries 1p *Wiltshire Record Office*

34170 Sir Harold Brakspear and Oswald Brakspear, architects: business records 15pp *Wiltshire Record Office*

34171 Wiltshire baptist churches 5pp *Wiltshire Record Office*

34172 Florence Nightingale: corresp and papers 53pp *Greater London Record Office and History Library*

34173 Nation Life Insurance Co Ltd 4pp *Greater London Record Office and History Library*

34174 Chesterfield College of Technology and Arts 4pp *Derbyshire Record Office*

34175 A & J Stewart Ltd, iron and steel tube mfrs, Glasgow and Coatbridge 5pp *City of Glasgow, Mitchell Library*

34176 Chester-le-Street Board of Guardians 3pp *Tyne and Wear Archives Service*

34177 Chester-le-Street Rural District Council 5pp *Tyne and Wear Archives Service*

34178 Chester-le-Street Board of Guardians 19pp *Durham County Record Office*

34179 Sunderland County Petty Sessions 4pp *Tyne and Wear Archives Service*

34180 Valletta: St Paul's Pro-Cathedral 29pp *Private*

34181 Durham County Association of Trades Councils 40pp *Durham County Record Office*

34182 Queens Own Royal West Kent Regiment 43pp *Centre for Kentish Studies*

34183 John Robson (Shipley) Ltd, diesel engine mfrs 20pp *West Yorkshire Archive Service, Bradford*

34184 Powell Brothers Ltd, mechanical engineers, Wrexham 2pp *National Library of Wales, Department of Manuscripts and Records*

34185 Montagu-Douglas-Scott family, Dukes of Buccleuch: Warwickshire estate papers 1p *Warwickshire County Record Office*

34186 Coventry Guild of the Holy Trinity: register[1] 170pp *Coventry City Record Office*

34187 Spencer Perceval, statesman: corresp and papers 31pp *Cambridge University Library, Department of Manuscripts and University Archives*

34188 Conwy and Colwyn Bay Joint Water and Supply Board 38pp *Gwynedd Archives and Museums Service, Caernarfon Area Record Office*

34189 Sutton manor records 13pp *Sutton Central Library*

34190 Webb family, stonemasons, Linton: business and family papers 17pp *Hereford Record Office*

34191 Carshalton manor records 30pp *Sutton Central Library*

34192 Sutton Public Hall Co Ltd 4pp *Sutton Central Library*

34193 Sutton Central Library: misc accessions 58pp *Sutton Central Library*

34194 Sutton Congregational Church 11pp *Sutton Central Library*

34195 Beddington: Royal Female Orphanage 1p *Sutton Central Library*

34196 AE Andrews & Son (West Bromwich) Ltd, blacksmiths and general mfrs 7pp *Sandwell District Libraries*

34197 William Stallworthy & Son, millers and animal feed stuff mfrs, Ampney Crucis 2pp *Gloucestershire Record Office*

34198 William Arthur Aickman, architect: corresp and papers 15pp *British Architectural Library*

34199 Architects Benevolent Society 3pp *British Architectural Library*

34200 Architectural Union Co Ltd, London 6pp *British Architectural Library*

34201 Sir Ove Nyquist Arup, civil engineer: papers rel to Modern Architectural Research Group 10pp *British Architectural Library*

34202 Sir Herbert Baker, architect: corresp and papers 37pp *British Architectural Library*

---

[1]Mary Dormer Harris (ed): *The Register of the Guild of the Holy Trinity, St Mary, St John the Baptist and St Katherine of Coventry*, 1935

34203　Sir Charles Barry, architect: corresp and papers incl papers of Charles Barry junior 12pp *British Architectural Library*

34204　William Walter Begley, architect, historian and ecclesiologist: corresp and autograph collection 6pp *British Architectural Library*

34205　John Bilson, architect, antiquarian and architectural writer: notebooks and misc papers 10pp *British Architectural Library*

34206　British Institute of Industrial Art 26pp *British Architectural Library*

34207　Arthur Stanley George Butler, architect and author: personal and family corresp and papers 8pp *British Architectural Library*

34208　Sir William Chambers, architect: corresp and papers 20pp *British Architectural Library*

34209　Wells Wintemute Coates, architect and designer: corresp and papers 3pp *British Architectural Library*

34210　Charles Robert Cockerell, architect: corresp and papers 33pp *British Architectural Library*

34211　Sir John Ninian Comper, architect: corresp and papers 94pp *British Architectural Library*

34212　John Gregory Crace, architectural decorator: corresp and accounts with AWN Pugin 6pp *British Architectural Library*

34213　Thomas Leverton Donaldson, architect, antiquarian and archaeologist: corresp and papers 7pp *British Architectural Library*

34214　Ecclesiological Society 10pp *British Architectural Library*

34215　Edward William Godwin, architect and antiquarian: papers 17pp *British Architectural Library*

34216　Harry Stuart Goodhart-Rendel, architect: corresp and papers 58pp *British Architectural Library*

34217　Charles Handley-Read, art historian and collector: corresp and working papers 25pp *British Architectural Library*

34218　Oliver Hill, architect: corresp and papers 90pp *British Architectural Library*

34219　Henry Holland, architect: corresp and papers 12pp *British Architectural Library*

34220　James Kennedy-Hawkes, architect: corresp and papers 2pp *British Architectural Library*

34221　London Architectural Society 2pp *British Architectural Library*

34222　Sir Edwin Landseer Lutyens, architect: family corresp and misc papers 273pp *British Architectural Library*

34223　Sir Edward Maufe, architect: corresp and papers 58pp *British Architectural Library*

34224　John Nash, architect: accounts 11pp *British Architectural Library*

34225　Coventry: Cappers' Company 2pp *Coventry City Record Office*

34226　William Newton, architect: corresp and papers 9pp *British Architectural Library*

34227　Wyatt Angelicus Van Sandau Papworth, architect and antiquary: corresp and papers 29pp *British Architectural Library*

34228　Harry Hardy Peach, furniture manufacturer: corresp and papers 25pp *British Architectural Library*

34229　Francis Cranmer Penrose, architect, archaeologist and astronomer: papers rel to Wellington monument, St Pauls Cathedral 20pp *British Architectural Library*

34230　Arthur Beresford Pite, architect: corresp and lecture notes 14pp *British Architectural Library*

34231　Halsey Ralph Ricardo, architect, designer and interior decorator: out-letter book 27pp *British Architectural Library*

34232　Thomas Rickman, architect and architectural writer: diaries 1p *British Architectural Library*

34233　Sebastopol: Penry Memorial Congregational Church 2pp *Gwent County Record Office*

34234　Gilwern United Reformed Church 6pp *Gwent County Record Office*

34235 Pontypool: Mountpleasant United Reformed Church 1p *Gwent County Record Office*

34236 Harry William Roberts and Arthur Leonard Roberts, architects: corresp and papers 3pp *British Architectural Library*

34237 Beaufort: Carmel Congregational Church 1p *Gwent County Record Office*

34238 Royal Institute of British Architects: prize and scholarship papers 34pp *British Architectural Library*

34239 Godfrey Herbert Samuel, architect: corresp and papers 80pp *British Architectural Library*

34240 Adrian Gilbert Scott, architect: office papers 3pp *British Architectural Library*

34241 Charles Marriott Oldrid Scott, architect: office papers 8pp *British Architectural Library*

34242 Sir George Gilbert Scott, architect: corresp and papers 8pp *British Architectural Library*

34243 George Gilbert Scott junior, architect: corresp and papers 18pp *British Architectural Library*

34244 Sir Giles Gilbert Scott, architect: corresp and papers 81pp *British Architectural Library*

34245 John Oldrid Scott, architect: corresp and papers 28pp *British Architectural Library*

34246 Richard Norman Shaw, architect: family corresp and accounts 9pp *British Architectural Library*

34247 Marshall Arnott Sisson, architect: corresp and papers 46pp *British Architectural Library*

34248 George John Skipper, architect: note-and-sketch books 4pp *British Architectural Library*

34249 Smirke family, painters and architects: corresp and papers 15pp *British Architectural Library*

34250 Soane Testimonial Committee 2pp *British Architectural Library*

34251 Society of Architects 20pp *British Architectural Library*

34252 Hugh Hutton Stannus, architect and designer: corresp and papers 28pp *British Architectural Library*

34253 Philip Armstrong Tilden, architect and writer: corresp and papers 7pp *British Architectural Library*

34254 Nantyglo: Bethlehem English Baptist Church 3pp *Gwent County Record Office*

34255 North Gwent Hospital Management Committee 2pp *Gwent County Record Office*

34256 Gwent Baptist marriage registers 4pp *Gwent County Record Office*

34257 Michaelstone-y-Fedw: Tirzah Baptist Church 1p *Gwent County Record Office*

34258 Magor Baptist Church 1p *Gwent County Record Office*

34259 Garndiffaith: Bethel Primitive Methodist Church 1p *Gwent County Record Office*

34260 Ford & Moore Ltd, ironmongers, Newport 2pp *Gwent County Record Office*

34261 Thomas Hewertson & Co, wholesale tobacconists, Newport 2pp *Gwent County Record Office*

34262 AJ Jacobs & Sons, pawnbrokers, Newport 2pp *Gwent County Record Office*

34263 John Basham & Sons, nurserymen and florists, Bassaleg 4pp *Gwent County Record Office*

34264 GC Clench, garage owner and confectioner, Usk 2pp *Gwent County Record Office*

34265 Sir Raymond Unwin, architect and town planner: corresp and working papers 16pp *British Architectural Library*

34266 Charles Francis Annesley Voysey, architect and designer: papers 2pp *British Architectural Library*

34267 Lewis Vulliamy, architect: corresp and office papers 81pp *British Architectural Library*

34268 Frederick Arthur Walters, architect: office papers 6pp *British Architectural Library*

34269 Cwmbran Development Corporation 380pp *Gwent County Record Office*

34270 Alfred Waterhouse, architect: letter books and misc papers 20pp *British Architectural Library*

34271 Stephen Walsh, architect and architectural historian: corresp and working papers 22pp *British Architectural Library*

34272 Sir Christopher Wren, architect: papers 11pp *British Architectural Library*

34273 Winchester: Hospital of St Mary Magdalene 16pp *Hampshire Record Office*

34274 Wyatt family, architects and sculptors: corresp and papers 21pp *British Architectural Library*

34275 British Architectural Library: misc accessions 250pp *British Architectural Library*

34276 Welsh Water Authority, Anglesey: records of predecessor bodies 8pp *Gwynedd Archives and Museums Service, Llangefni Area Record Office*

34277 Canterbury Cathedral: Dean and Chapter estate papers 178pp *Canterbury City and Cathedral Archives*

34278 Denbighshire and Flintshire Agricultural Society 3pp *Clwyd Record Office, Hawarden Branch*

34279 Flintshire co-operative societies 2pp *Clwyd Record Office, Hawarden Branch*

34280 W Williams & Son, printers and publishers, Holywell 3pp *Clwyd Record Office, Hawarden Branch*

34281 Lindsay-Bethune family, Earls of Lindsay: family and estate papers 39pp *Scottish Record Office*

34282 Ogilvy family, baronets, of Inverquharity: family and estate papers 80pp *Scottish Record Office*

34283 Hawarden Institute 2pp *Clwyd Record Office, Hawarden Branch*

34284 Chester, Wrexham & North Wales Savings Bank, Mold branch 2pp *Clwyd Record Office, Hawarden Branch*

34285 Bodelwyddan: Lowther College 6pp *Clwyd Record Office, Hawarden Branch*

34286 Denbigh Water Co 2pp *Clwyd Record Office, Ruthin Branch*

34287 Clwyd Record Office, Ruthin branch: misc accessions 22pp *Clwyd Record Office, Ruthin Branch*

34288 Ruabon Brick and Terracotta Co Ltd 3pp *Clwyd Record Office, Ruthin Branch*

34289 Wrexham Trades Council and Divisional Labour Party 1p *Clwyd Record Office, Ruthin Branch*

34290 Wrexham Savings Bank 2pp *Clwyd Record Office, Ruthin Branch*

34291 James Idwal Jones MP: corresp and papers 5pp *Clwyd Record Office, Ruthin Branch*

34292 Carruthers family of Holmains: family and estate papers 14pp *Scottish Record Office*

34293 Powell Brothers Ltd, mechanical engineers, Wrexham 9pp *Clwyd Record Office, Ruthin Branch*

34294 New Quay Urban District Council 4pp *Dyfed Archives Service, Cardiganshire Area Record Office*

34295 Aberystwyth crew lists and agreements 20pp *Dyfed Archives Service, Cardiganshire Area Record Office*

34296 Morgan and Gwynne families of Carmarthen: Morgan and Barnsfield estate deeds and papers 62pp *Dyfed Archives Service, Carmarthenshire Area Record Office*

34297 Cardiganshire Territorial and Auxiliary Forces Association 2pp *Dyfed Archives Service, Cardiganshire Area Record Office*

34298 General Refractories Ltd: records of Ewloe Barn and Old Ewloe brick and tile works 3pp *Clwyd Record Office, Hawarden Branch*

34299 John Fox & Co, brewers, Ewloe 5pp *Clwyd Record Office, Hawarden Branch*

34300 Matthew Francis & Son, mining engineers, Halkyn 6pp *Clwyd Record Office, Hawarden Branch*

34301 Carmarthenshire boards of guardians 1p *Dyfed Archives Service, Carmarthenshire Area Record Office*

34302 JR Phillips & Co Ltd, wine and spirit merchants, Bristol 14pp *Bristol Record Office*

34303 Bristol: Clifton High School for Girls 9pp *Bristol Record Office*

34304 Curtis, Jenkins, Cornwell & Co, chartered accountants, Bristol 13pp *Bristol Record Office*

34305 West Mendip Methodist Circuit 17pp *Bristol Record Office*

34306 Swaffham Baptist Church 7pp *Norfolk Record Office*

34307 Purdy & Holley, solicitors, Reepham 4pp *Norfolk Record Office*

34308 Panthowell estate: deeds and papers 17pp *Dyfed Archives Service, Carmarthenshire Area Record Office*

34309 Haslam Foundry & Engineering Co Ltd, electrical and refrigeration machinery mfrs, Derby 1p *Derbyshire Record Office*

34310 Pickersgill & Frost Ltd, grate mfrs, Langley Mill 4pp *Derbyshire Record Office*

34311 Bryan Donkin Co Ltd, mechanical and gas engineers and valve mfrs, Chesterfield 5pp *Derbyshire Record Office*

*34312 Webster family, baronets, of Battle Abbey: family and estate papers incl monastic and manorial records 478pp *Huntington Library*

34313 Mansel family, baronets, of Muddlescombe and Trimsaran: deeds and papers 44pp *Dyfed Archives Service, Carmarthenshire Area Record Office*

34314 Goldsworthy Lowes Dickinson, historian and philosophical writer: corresp and papers incl literary MSS 26pp *Cambridge University: Kings College Modern Records Centre*

34315 Haverfordwest: Albany United Reformed Church 3pp *Dyfed Archives Service, Pembrokeshire Area Record Office*

34316 Pembroke Board of Guardians 9pp *Dyfed Archives Service, Pembrokeshire Area Record Office*

34317 Fishguard and Goodwick Urban District Council 41pp *Dyfed Archives Service, Pembrokeshire Area Record Office*

34318 Sumner, Harker & Co Ltd, machinery exporters, Manchester 31pp *Manchester Central Library, Local Studies Unit*

34319 Harvey & Wheeler, estate agents, London 121pp *Liverpool University Archives Unit*

34320 Lt-General Sir William Howley Goodenough: corresp rel to Gordon relief expedition 4pp *Durham University Library, Archives and Special Collections*

34321 Graham Dudley Lampen, colonial administrator: corresp and papers 22pp *Durham University Library, Archives and Special Collections*

34322 Brigadier-General Sir Gilbert Falkingham Clayton: corresp and papers 33pp *Durham University Library, Archives and Special Collections*

34323 David Molyneux Hardy Evans, colonial administrator: corresp and papers 31pp *Durham University Library, Archives and Special Collections*

34324 Sir James Angus Gillan, colonial administrator: corresp and papers 47pp *Durham University Library, Archives and Special Collections*

34325 Brigadier John Hatton Rolt Orlebar: corresp and papers rel to Sudan Defence Force 22pp *Durham University Library, Archives and Special Collections*

34326 Allan James Vincent Arthur, colonial administrator: corresp and papers 7pp *Durham University Library, Archives and Special Collections*

34327 Geoffrey Herbert Barter, colonial administrator: corresp and papers 9pp *Durham University Library, Archives and Special Collections*

34328 Sir Gawain Westray Bell, colonial administrator: corresp and papers 16pp *Durham University Library, Archives and Special Collections*

34329 John Henry Dick, colonial administrator: diaries and photographs 6pp *Durham University Library, Archives and Special Collections*

34330 John Longe, colonial administrator: corresp and papers 14pp *Durham University Library, Archives and Special Collections*

34331 Paul James Sandison, colonial administrator: corresp and papers 18pp *Durham University Library, Archives and Special Collections*

34332 Warde-Norbury family of Hooton Pagnell: family and estate papers 60pp *Doncaster Archives Department*

34333 Alexander Rollo Colin Bolton, colonial administrator: corresp and papers 12pp *Durham University Library, Archives and Special Collections*

34334 Major-General John Fielden Brocklehurst, Baron Ranksborough: corresp and papers rel to the Sudan 4pp *Durham University Library, Archives and Special Collections*

34335 Mabel E Wolff, Inspector of Midwives in the Sudan: corresp and papers 35pp *Durham University Library, Archives and Special Collections*

34336 Brian Apcar Carlisle, colonial administrator and oil company executive: corresp and papers 5pp *Durham University Library, Archives and Special Collections*

34337 Jardine family, baronets, of Applegirth: family and estate papers 58pp *Private*

34338 Scottish Co-operative Women's Guild: Kinning Park branch 4pp *Strathclyde Regional Archives*

34339 Cape-Bretoniana Archives: MS collections 50pp *Cape-Bretoniana Archives*

34340 Charity Commission: Merseyside charities accounts 18pp *Merseyside Record Office*

34341 Dundee: Rattray Street Baptist Church 5pp *Dundee District Archive and Record Centre*

34342 Brooklands Museum: MS collections 12pp *Brooklands Museum*

34343 Merseyside Fire Service: records of predecessor bodies 64pp *Merseyside Record Office*

34344 Frank Pick, transport manager: papers 18pp *London Transport Museum*

34345 Birkenhead Constituency Labour Party 2pp *Merseyside Record Office*

34346 Vane family, Barons Barnard: family and estate papers 397pp *Private*

34347 Toxteth Constituency Labour Party 1p *Merseyside Record Office*

34348 Association of Religious Agencies in Liverpool 1p *Merseyside Record Office*

34349 Bowen family of Llwyngwair: family and estate papers incl those of Bevan family of Laugharne 434pp *National Library of Wales, Department of Manuscripts and Records*

34350 Wallasey: New Brighton United Reformed Church 4pp *Merseyside Record Office*

*34351 John Strachey, Labour politician and socialist thinker: corresp and papers 9pp *Private*

34352 Salusbury family, baronets, of Lleweni: deeds and papers 212pp *National Library of Wales, Department of Manuscripts and Records*

34353 British Association for the Advancement of Science: Merseyside area 2pp *Merseyside Record Office*

34354 Crosby: Blundellsands Methodist Church 3pp *Merseyside Record Office*

34355 DJ MacDonald Ltd, textile machinery mfrs and mill furnishers, Dundee 21pp *Dundee University Library, Archives and Manuscripts Department*

34356 Durham University Library Sudan Archive: MS collections 162pp *Durham University Library, Archives and Special Collections*

34357 Dugdale family of Llwyn: deeds and papers incl those of Humffreys family 304pp *National Library of Wales, Department of Manuscripts and Records*

34358 Muscular Dystrophy Group of Great Britain: Merseyside branch 1p *Merseyside Record Office*

34359 Liverpool: Trinity Orrell Park United Reformed Church 4pp *Merseyside Record Office*

34360 Windsor-Clive family, Earls of Plymouth: deeds 301pp *National Library of Wales, Department of Manuscripts and Records*

34361 John Montgomery Traherne, Glamorgan antiquary: corresp and papers 221pp *National Library of Wales, Department of Manuscripts and Records*

34362 Staffordshire Federation of Womens Institutes 10pp *Staffordshire Record Office*

34363 Great Wyrley Colliery Co Ltd 3pp *Staffordshire Record Office*

34364 CM Bass & Son, chemists, Rugeley 1p *Staffordshire Record Office*

34365 Association of Friends of Cannock Chase 1p *Staffordshire Record Office*

34366 Staffordshire Methodist circuit plans 3pp *Staffordshire Record Office*

34367 National Farmers Union: Staffordshire County branch 3pp *Staffordshire Record Office*

34368 Stoke-on-Trent City General Hospital 1p *Staffordshire Record Office*

34369 Brocklehurst family, baronets, of Swythamley: estate papers 20pp *Staffordshire Record Office*

34370 Burton upon Trent Board of Guardians 10pp *Burton upon Trent Public Library*

34371 Burton upon Trent Society of Coopers 3pp *Burton upon Trent Public Library*

34372 Winterton & Sons, auctioneers and valuers, Lichfield: field books 4pp *Lichfield Joint Record Office*

34373 Lichfield: Dr Milley's Hospital 6pp *Lichfield Joint Record Office*

34374 Amalgamated Union of Building Trade Workers: Lichfield branch 2pp *Lichfield Joint Record Office*

34375 Huddleston family of Sawston Hall: corresp 180pp *County Record Office, Cambridge*

34376 Crosby (Wesleyan) Mission Church 3pp *Merseyside Record Office*

34377 Waterloo Methodist Church, Birchdale Road 2pp *Merseyside Record Office*

34378 Invergarry Iron Works 2pp *Scottish Record Office*

34379 Amos Atkinson Ltd, shoe makers and retailers, Newcastle upon Tyne 2pp *Tyne and Wear Archives Service*

34380 Ticehurst House Hospital 62pp *Wellcome Institute for the History of Medicine*

34381 Independent Order of Oddfellows, Manchester Unity: Lichfield (Dr Johnson) lodge 3pp *Lichfield Joint Record Office*

34382 Herbert Grainger, local historian: working papers and collected MSS 5pp *William Salt Library*

34383 Staffordshire Baptist marriage registers 1p *Staffordshire Record Office*

*34384 James Jurin, physician and secretary of the Royal Society: corresp 25pp *Wellcome Institute for the History of Medicine*

34385 Burslem: Church of Christ Meeting House 1p *Staffordshire Record Office*

34386 Dublin: Ralph Macklin schools 2pp *Representative Church Body Library*

34387 Shotts Iron Co Ltd, ironfounders and coal masters 5pp *Scottish Record Office*

34388 Association for the Relief of Distressed Protestants, Dublin 2pp *Representative Church Body Library*

34389 Meath Church Choral Association 2pp *Representative Church Body Library*

34390 Meath Protestant Orphan Society 2pp *Representative Church Body Library*

34391 Dobbie McInnes Ltd, scientific instrument mfrs, Glasgow 2pp *Scottish Record Office*

34392 Sir James Stephen, civil servant and historian, and Sir James Fitzjames Stephen, judge: corresp and misc family papers 11pp *Representative Church Body Library*

34393 Portsea Island Mutual Co-operative Society Ltd 12pp *Portsmouth City Records Office*

34394 Barnstaple Board of Guardians 2pp *North Devon Record Office*

34395 Parker family, Earls of Morley: corresp 210pp *West Devon Area Record Office*

34396 Brixton Feoffee Lands Charity 16pp *West Devon Area Record Office*

34397 Portsmouth: Cosham Society of Arts and Sports, ballroom dancing section 1p *Portsmouth City Records Office*

34398 HG Fox, teacher: diaries and papers incl those of his wife 30pp *Portsmouth City Records Office*

34399 Jones Brothers (Holloway) Ltd, department store, London 5pp *Private*

34400 Ivybridge: Didworthy Sanatorium Lee Mill Hospital 9pp *West Devon Area Record Office*

34401 Torrington Industrial Co-operative Society Ltd 1p *North Devon Record Office*

34402 Pitts Tuckers, solicitors, Barnstaple: records incl clients papers 35pp *North Devon Record Office*

34403 Sunderland: Cleveland Road Methodist Church 6pp *Tyne and Wear Archives Service*

34404 Preston family of Moreby Hall: deeds and papers 141pp *Hull University, Brynmor Jones Library*

34405 Tavistock Cottage Hospital 5pp *West Devon Area Record Office*

34406 Newcastle upon Tyne: Westgate Road Baptist Church 1p *Tyne and Wear Archives Service*

34407 Winlaton United Reformed Church 5pp *Tyne and Wear Archives Service*

34408 Sunderland: Westmoor Road Methodist Church, Pallion 5pp *Tyne and Wear Archives Service*

34409 Sunderland First Primitive Methodist Circuit 6pp *Tyne and Wear Archives Service*

34410 Sunderland: Mount Tabor Methodist Church, Chester Road 4pp *Tyne and Wear Archives Service*

34411 John Barnes & Co Ltd, department store, London 3pp *Private*

34412 Sunderland South Methodist Circuit 9pp *Tyne and Wear Archives Service*

34413 Sunderland: Thornhill Methodist Church 5pp *Tyne and Wear Archives Service*

*34414 Nikolaas Tinbergen, ethologist: corresp and papers 90pp *Oxford University: Bodleian Library, Department of Western Manuscripts*

34415 Williams-Drummond family, baronets, of Edwinsford: deeds and estate papers 1055pp *National Library of Wales, Department of Manuscripts and Records*

34416 Rear-Admiral Noel Wright: diaries and misc papers 5pp *Private*

34417 Rice family, Barons Dynevor: deeds and papers 184pp *National Library of Wales, Department of Manuscripts and Records*

34418 George Frederic Watts, painter and sculptor: corresp 12pp *National Portrait Gallery Archive and Library*

34419 Webley Parry family of Noyadd Trefawr: deeds and papers incl those of Lewes family of Gellydywyll 396pp *National Library of Wales, Department of Manuscripts and Records*

34420 Charles and John Watkins, photographers: corresp and papers 5pp *National Portrait Gallery Archive and Library*

34421 Hugh Fraser Stewart, French scholar: personal and family corresp and papers 26pp *Cambridge University Library, Department of Manuscripts and University Archives*

34422 William Dillwyn, Quaker merchant: diaries 225pp *National Library of Wales, Department of Manuscripts and Records*

34423 Benjamin Flower, political writer: corresp with his wife 27pp *National Library of Wales, Department of Manuscripts and Records*

34424 Gee & Son Ltd, printers, Denbigh 44pp *National Library of Wales, Department of Manuscripts and Records*

34425 Lewis Weston Dillwyn, naturalist: diaries and misc papers 567pp *National Library of Wales, Department of Manuscripts and Records*

34426 Hugh Emlyn Hooson, Baron Hooson: corresp and papers 17pp *National Library of Wales, Department of Manuscripts and Records*

34427 William Griffiths, Calvinistic Methodist minister: corresp, journals and diaries 6pp *National Library of Wales, Department of Manuscripts and Records*

34428 Winlaton: Norman's Riding Hospital 3pp *Tyne and Wear Archives Service*

34429 Herbert Stanley Jevons, economist: corresp and papers 29pp *National Library of Wales, Department of Manuscripts and Records*

34430 John Jenkins, Resolven and Neath antiquary: MS collection 66pp *National Library of Wales, Department of Manuscripts and Records*

34431 General Electric Company plc 7pp *Private*

34432 Edward Barnard & Sons Ltd, silversmiths, London 22pp *Victoria & Albert Museum, Archive of Art and Design*

34433 Paul Diverres: MSS and notes on celtic languages 52pp *National Library of Wales, Department of Manuscripts and Records*

34434 Llanidloes Borough 12pp *National Library of Wales, Department of Manuscripts and Records*

34435 Sunderland: Thornhill United Methodist Circuit 1p *Tyne and Wear Archives Service*

34436 John Lloyd, historian: MS collection rel to the iron industry 54pp *National Library of Wales, Department of Manuscripts and Records*

34437 North Shields: Moor Park Hospital 1p *Tyne and Wear Archives Service*

34438 Newcastle upon Tyne: The Gables Maternity Hospital 2pp *Tyne and Wear Archives Service*

34439 Lynton Harold Lamb, graphic artist: corresp and papers 10pp *Victoria & Albert Museum, Archive of Art and Design*

34440 Sunderland West Methodist Circuit 2pp *Tyne and Wear Archives Service*

34441 John Gibson, sculptor: letters to Henry Sandbach and his wife 37pp *National Library of Wales, Department of Manuscripts and Records*

34442 Ryhope Colliery: Taylor Street Methodist Church 2pp *Tyne and Wear Archives Service*

34443 Lachasse Ltd, ladies tailors, London 12pp *Victoria & Albert Museum, Archive of Art and Design*

34444 David Davies, MP and industrialist: corresp and papers 48pp *National Library of Wales, Department of Manuscripts and Records*

34445 John E Day, ironmongers, Chelmsford 8pp *Essex Record Office*

34446 Nelson and Edith Dawson, silversmiths and decorative artists: corresp, papers and designs 11pp *Victoria & Albert Museum, Archive of Art and Design*

34447 SG Swayne Ltd, production engineers, Ilford 10pp *Essex Record Office*

34448 Evans & Bevan Ltd, colliery proprietors, Neath 11pp *National Library of Wales, Department of Manuscripts and Records*

34449 Eve Sandford, knitting designer: designs and samples 2pp *Victoria & Albert Museum, Archive of Art and Design*

34450 Halstead: St Francis of Assisi Roman Catholic Church 3pp *Essex Record Office*

34451 Stock Congregational Church 4pp *Essex Record Office*

34452 J Clarke, furniture mfrs, High Wycombe 125pp *Victoria & Albert Museum, Archive of Art and Design*

34453 Hall, Russell & Co Ltd, shipbuilders and marine engineers, Aberdeen: drawings 3pp *Aberdeen Art Gallery and Museum*

34454 William Dyce, painter: corresp and papers incl biographical material collected by his son 3pp *Aberdeen Art Gallery and Museum*

34455 Marie Stevenson, needlework teacher: illustrated diaries 2pp *Victoria & Albert Museum, Archive of Art and Design*

34456 Elizabeth Hake, researcher on quilting: corresp and papers 43pp *Victoria & Albert Museum, Archive of Art and Design*

34457 Ernest Heasman, stained glass artist: designs and papers 10pp *Victoria & Albert Museum, Archive of Art and Design*

34458 Helen Megaw, crystallographer: corresp and papers 10pp *Victoria & Albert Museum, Archive of Art and Design*

34459 Sunderland: Durham Road Methodist Church 2pp *Tyne and Wear Archives Service*

34460 Sunderland: Hendon Methodist Church 5pp *Tyne and Wear Archives Service*

34461 Sunderland: Mainsforth Terrace Methodist Church, Hendon 2pp *Tyne and Wear Archives Service*

34462 Sunderland: Sans Street Methodist Church 4pp *Tyne and Wear Archives Service*

34463 Sunderland: South Durham Street United Methodist Church 2pp *Tyne and Wear Archives Service*

34464 Sunderland: Wesley Hall Mission, Trimdon Street 2pp *Tyne and Wear Archives Service*

34465 Sunderland: Whitburn Street Methodist Church 2pp *Tyne and Wear Archives Service*

34466 Sunderland: Vicarage Lane Methodist Church, Ford 2pp *Tyne and Wear Archives Service*

34467 Bernhard Baer, publisher: corresp and papers rel to Ganymed Press 63pp *Victoria & Albert Museum, Archive of Art and Design*

34468 Gregynog estate rentals and account books 5pp *National Library of Wales, Department of Manuscripts and Records*

34469 Newcastle upon Tyne: Bewick Street Baptist Church 1p *Tyne and Wear Archives Service*

34470 Newcastle upon Tyne Savings Bank: West Chirton branch 4pp *Tyne and Wear Archives Service*

34471 WW & R Johnson & Sons, lead mfrs, London 3pp *Tyne and Wear Archives Service*

34472 Lee family of Dinas Powis: deeds and estate papers 56pp *National Library of Wales, Department of Manuscripts and Records*

34473 Longueville & Co, solicitors, Oswestry: client's papers 136pp *National Library of Wales, Department of Manuscripts and Records*

34474 WH Smith & Co (Whitchurch) Ltd, agricultural engineers and ironfounders 4pp *Shropshire Records and Research Unit*

34475 C & W Walker Ltd, gas engineers, Donnington 2pp *Shropshire Records and Research Unit*

34476 Tooker family of Hinton: deeds and papers 4pp *Hampshire Record Office*

34477 Birmingham Battery & Metal Co Ltd, copper and copper alloy product mfrs 21pp *Private*

34478 B & JC Pinniger, solicitors, Newbury: papers rel to the estates of the Herbert family, Earls of Carnarvon 19pp *Hampshire Record Office*

34479 Raleigh Industries Ltd, bicycle mfrs, Nottingham 88pp[1] *Nottinghamshire Archives Office*

34480 London: Albert Dock Seamen's Hospital 5pp *Royal London Hospital Archives Centre and Museum*

34481 Henry Balfour & Co Ltd, engineers and processing plant mfrs, Leven 16pp *Scottish Record Office*

34482 Sunderland: South Durham Street United Methodist Mission Circuit 1p *Tyne and Wear Archives Service*

34483 John Wyatt, industrialist and inventor: corresp and papers 2pp *Birmingham Central Library, Archives Division*

34484 Newman & Appleby, land and estate agents, Fareham 30pp *Hampshire Record Office*

34485 George Heaton, inventor: corresp and papers rel to his steam carriage 1p *Birmingham Central Library, Archives Division*

---

[1]A Millward: *The Raleigh Archive a detailed list of the contents*

34486 Winchester Rural Deanery 1p
Hampshire Record Office

34487 Bordon Roman Catholic
Church 1p *Hampshire Record
Office*

34488 Ringwood Unitarian Church
1p *Hampshire Record Office*

34489 Kingsclere charities 14pp
Hampshire Record Office

34490 Samuel Denison & Son Ltd,
testing machine mfrs, Leeds
1p *West Yorkshire Archive
Service, Leeds*

34491 Deightons Patent Flue & Tube
Co Ltd, boiler flue mfrs,
Leeds 4pp *West Yorkshire
Archive Service, Leeds*

34492 Yorkshire Patent Steam
Wagon Co, Leeds 4pp *West
Yorkshire Archive Service, Leeds*

34493 Frost family of West
Wratting: misc corresp and
papers 23pp *County Record
Office, Cambridge*

34494 Thomas Smith & Sons
(Rodley) Ltd, crane builders
1p *West Yorkshire Archive
Service, Leeds*

34495 Grimsby Methodist Circuit
57pp *Lincolnshire Archives*

34496 Bertie Edward Parker Leighton
MP: Sweeney Hall MS
collection 65pp *National
Library of Wales, Department of
Manuscripts and Records*

34497 Letchworth Free Church 10pp
Hertfordshire Record Office

34498 Adeyfield Free Church 3pp
Hertfordshire Record Office

34499 Ware United Reformed
Church 7pp *Hertfordshire
Record Office*

34500 Royston United Reformed
Church 6pp *Hertfordshire
Record Office*

34501 Radlett United Reformed
Church 5pp *Hertfordshire
Record Office*

34502 Wheathamstead United
Reformed Church 4pp
Hertfordshire Record Office

34503 Harry McShane, socialist:
corresp with Raya
Dunayevskaya and misc papers
54pp *National Museum of
Labour History*

34504 Chelmsford: League of Friends
of St John's Hospital 6pp
Essex Record Office

34505 Bishop Auckland Constituency
Labour Party 12pp *Durham
County Record Office*

34506 Chelmsford District
Association of Leagues of
Hospital Friends 4pp *Essex
Record Office*

34507 Medway Towns Methodist
Circuit 125pp *Medway Area
Archives Office*

34508 Loughton Lopping
Endowment Fund 12pp *Essex
Record Office*

34509 Independent Order of
Oddfellows, Manchester
Unity: Tillingham, Colchester
and Maldon district 'Welcome
Home' lodge 9pp *Essex Record
Office*

34510 Soroptimist International:
Chelmsford club 4pp *Essex
Record Office*

34511 Labour Party Eastern Region
Executive Committee 2pp
Essex Record Office

34512 Charles Lane & Sons Ltd, nail
mfrs, Leeds 1p *West Yorkshire
Archive Service, Leeds*

34513 Rice & Co (Leeds) Ltd,
hydraulic engineers 2pp *West
Yorkshire Archive Service, Leeds*

34514 Reynolds & Branson Ltd,
manufacturing chemists and
optical instrument mfrs, Leeds
1p *West Yorkshire Archive
Service, Leeds*

34515 Exminster: Exe Vale Hospital
80pp *Devon Record Office*

34516 Moreton Rural Deanery 1p
Devon Record Office

34517 Okehampton Rural Deanery
1p *Devon Record Office*

34518 Yarcombe Baptist Church 1p
Devon Record Office

34519 Pembrey Wesleyan Methodist
Chapel 1p *Dyfed Archives
Service, Carmarthenshire Area
Record Office*

34520 Salter family of Newlands
Farm, Broadclyst: business and
family papers 3pp *Devon
Record Office*

34521 Birmingham Gaol Sessions and
Magistrates' Courts 4pp
*Birmingham Central Library,
Archives Division*

34522 Yorkshire Switchgear &
Engineering Co Ltd, electrical
engineers, Leeds 2pp *West
Yorkshire Archive Service, Leeds*

34523 Paish & Co (1937) Ltd,
musical instrument dealers,
Torquay 1p *Devon Record
Office*

34524 Bisley Blue Coat School 3pp *Gloucestershire Record Office*

34525 Winchcombe Turnpike Trust 2pp *Gloucestershire Record Office*

34526 Cleeve and Evesham Turnpike Trust 4pp *Gloucestershire Record Office*

34527 Scott family, baronets, of Great Barr: deeds and papers 44pp *Birmingham Central Library, Archives Division*

34528 Little & Hutton, solicitors, Stroud: records incl clients papers 14pp *Gloucestershire Record Office*

34529 Meade family of Earsham Hall: family and estate papers incl Windham and Dalling families 200pp *Norfolk Record Office*

34530 HH Martyn & Co Ltd, architectural metal workers, Cheltenham 16pp *Gloucestershire Record Office*

34531 Stroud Subscription Rooms 1p *Gloucestershire Record Office*

34532 Birmingham: Digbeth Institute 1p *Birmingham Central Library, Archives Division*

34533 Birmingham: Stoney Lane Congregational Church 1p *Birmingham Central Library, Archives Division*

34534 Birmingham: Aston Manor Congregational Chapel 1p *Birmingham Central Library, Archives Division*

34535 Birmingham: Hay Mills Congregational Church 1p *Birmingham Central Library, Archives Division*

34536 Birmingham: Bournbrook Congregational Church 1p *Birmingham Central Library, Archives Division*

34537 Birmingham: Soho Hill Congregational Church, Handsworth 3pp *Birmingham Central Library, Archives Division*

34538 Association of Underwriters and Insurance Brokers in Glasgow 3pp *Strathclyde Regional Archives*

34539 Robert Dunn, surgeon: personal and family corresp 6pp *Wellcome Institute for the History of Medicine*

34540 Goldney family of Clifton: corresp and papers 6pp *Bristol University Library*

34541 Glasgow: Barony of Gorbals Benevolent Society 4pp *Strathclyde Regional Archives*

34542 Birmingham: Bristol Road Methodist Church, Northfield 5pp *Birmingham Central Library, Archives Division*

34543 Birmingham: Tyseley Methodist Church 2pp *Birmingham Central Library, Archives Division*

34544 Great Barr Methodist Church 1p *Birmingham Central Library, Archives Division*

34545 Elmore Womens Institute 1p *Gloucestershire Record Office*

34546 Staffordshire County Courts 1p *Staffordshire Record Office*

34547 Staffordshire and Uttoxeter Magistrates Court 2pp *Staffordshire Record Office*

34548 Cheddleton Parish Institute 1p *Staffordshire Record Office*

34549 Lichfield Municipal Charities 7pp *Lichfield Joint Record Office*

34550 Colchester: Lion Walk United Reformed Church 23pp *Essex Record Office, Colchester and North-East Essex Branch*

34551 Colchester: Harwich Road United Reformed Church 5pp *Essex Record Office, Colchester and North-East Essex Branch*

34552 Colchester Charity School 4pp *Essex Record Office, Colchester and North-East Essex Branch*

34553 Colchester Engineering Society 7pp *Essex Record Office, Colchester and North-East Essex Branch*

34554 FS Daniell & Son, auctioneers, estate and insurance agents, Colchester 33pp *Essex Record Office, Colchester and North-East Essex Branch*

34555 Transport and General Workers Union: Gloucester district 20pp *Gloucestershire Record Office*

34556 Middlewich Methodist Circuit 1p *Cheshire Record Office*

34557 Birmingham: Bradford Street Methodist Chapel 3pp *Birmingham Central Library, Archives Division*

34558 Birmingham: St Andrews Methodist Church, Stirchley 2pp *Birmingham Central Library, Archives Division*

34559 Birmingham: Shenley Hill Methodist Church, Northfield 4pp *Birmingham Central Library, Archives Division*

34560 Birmingham: Asbury Memorial Chapel, Handsworth 2pp *Birmingham Central Library, Archives Division*

34561 Birmingham: Sandon Road Methodist Church, Edgbaston 2pp *Birmingham Central Library, Archives Division*

34562 Birmingham: Central Hall, Corporation Street 9pp *Birmingham Central Library, Archives Division*

34563 Birmingham: California Methodist Church, Harborne 2pp *Birmingham Central Library, Archives Division*

34564 Birmingham: Harborne Methodist Church, South Street 5pp *Birmingham Central Library, Archives Division*

34565 Birmingham: Islington Methodist Church, Edgbaston 5pp *Birmingham Central Library, Archives Division*

34566 Great Barr: Pheasey Methodist Church 2pp *Birmingham Central Library, Archives Division*

34567 Birmingham: Newtown Row Methodist Church 2pp *Birmingham Central Library, Archives Division*

34568 Birmingham: Havergal House Methodist Church 2pp *Birmingham Central Library, Archives Division*

34569 Birmingham: Brookfields Methodist Church, Winson Green 2pp *Birmingham Central Library, Archives Division*

34570 Birmingham: Nechells Hall Methodist Church 4pp *Birmingham Central Library, Archives Division*

34571 Birmingham: Mansfield Road Methodist Church, Aston 3pp *Birmingham Central Library, Archives Division*

34572 Birmingham: Lichfield Road Methodist Church, Aston 2pp *Birmingham Central Library, Archives Division*

34573 Nether Whitacre Methodist Church 3pp *Birmingham Central Library, Archives Division*

34574 Birmingham: Holliday Street Mission Hall 2pp *Birmingham Central Library, Archives Division*

34575 Birmingham: College Road Methodist Church, Quinton 4pp *Birmingham Central Library, Archives Division*

34576 Birmingham: Cherry Street Methodist Chapel 8pp *Birmingham Central Library, Archives Division*

34577 Saltersford School 7pp *Cheshire Record Office*

34578 Birmingham: Trinity Methodist Church, Winson Green 2pp *Birmingham Central Library, Archives Division*

34579 Birmingham: Unett Street Methodist Church, Lozells 2pp *Birmingham Central Library, Archives Division*

34580 Birmingham: Washwood Heath Methodist Church, Saltley 7pp *Birmingham Central Library, Archives Division*

34581 Birmingham: Greet Methodist Church 1p *Birmingham Central Library, Archives Division*

34582 West Cheshire Coroners District 1p *Cheshire Record Office*

34583 Knutsford Grammar School 4pp *Cheshire Record Office*

34584 William Harold Hutchings, artist: sketchbooks and scrapbooks 6pp *Cheshire Record Office*

*34585 Augustus Edwin John, painter and etcher: corresp and papers 242pp *National Library of Wales, Department of Manuscripts and Records*

34586 Northleach Rural Deanery 2pp *Gloucestershire Record Office*

34587 Gloucestershire Constabulary 19pp *Gloucestershire Record Office*

34588 Blythe, Dutton & Holloway, solicitors, London: Gloucestershire clients papers 5pp *Gloucestershire Record Office*

34589 Cirencester: Ampney Sheephouse Farm 2pp *Gloucestershire Record Office*

34590 Booth United Reformed Church 2pp *West Yorkshire Archive Service, Calderdale*

34591 James Maxton MP: personal and family corresp and papers 33pp *Strathclyde Regional Archives*

34592 Birmingham Blue Coat School 9pp *Birmingham Central Library, Archives Division*

34593 William Mackenzie, cooper and timber merchant, Birmingham 5pp *Birmingham Central Library, Archives Division*

34594 George Winnall & Son Ltd, manufacturers agents, Birmingham 1p *Birmingham Central Library, Archives Division*

34595 Sheffield Equalized Independent Druids: Smethwick branch 1p *Birmingham Central Library, Archives Division*

34596 William Eric Harding, Congregational minister: diaries and papers 2pp *Birmingham Central Library, Archives Division*

34597 Halifax Nuclear Disarmament Group 11pp *West Yorkshire Archive Service, Calderdale*

34598 Mary Capper, Quaker: corresp and misc papers 8pp *Birmingham Central Library, Archives Division*

34599 Birmingham Stock Exchange 11pp *Birmingham Central Library, Archives Division*

34600 James Harrison & Sons Ltd, manufacturing jewellers, Birmingham 2pp *Birmingham Central Library, Archives Division*

34601 Birmingham Botanical and Horticultural Society 34pp *Birmingham Central Library, Archives Division*

34602 Scribbans's Purity Bread Ltd, Birmingham 1p *Birmingham Central Library, Archives Division*

34603 Sir Herbert John Baptista Manzoni, civil engineer: scrapbooks 2pp *Birmingham Central Library, Archives Division*

34604 Richard Peyton, musical patron: autograph scrapbook 8pp *Birmingham Central Library, Archives Division*

34605 East Worcestershire Conservative Association 1p *Birmingham Central Library, Archives Division*

34606 McKewan & McKewan, architects, Birmingham 4pp *Birmingham Central Library, Archives Division*

34607 Birmingham Hospitals Contributory Association 3pp *Birmingham Central Library, Archives Division*

34608 Cadbury Trusts 34pp *Birmingham Central Library, Archives Division*

34609 Max Bruch, composer: letters to Richard Peyton 2pp *Birmingham Central Library, Archives Division*

34610 Beacon Insurance Co Ltd, Birmingham 7pp *Birmingham Central Library, Archives Division*

34611 Liverpool: Rankin Memorial Presbyterian Church, Norris Green 2pp *Merseyside Record Office*

34612 Birmingham: Sir Josiah Mason's Orphanage and Almhouses 18pp *Birmingham Central Library, Archives Division*

34613 Rubery Hill Mental Hospital 4pp *Birmingham Central Library, Archives Division*

34614 Birmingham: Bourne College 2pp *Birmingham Central Library, Archives Division*

34615 Dundee: HMS Unicorn Preservation Society 23pp *Private*

34616 Birmingham mental hospitals 2pp *Birmingham Central Library, Archives Division*

34617 Christie-Miller family of Craigentinny: family and estate papers 9pp *City of Edinburgh District Council Archives*

34618 London Head Teachers Association 15pp *Greater London Record Office and History Library*

34619 London: Royal Chest Hospital 13pp *Greater London Record Office and History Library*

34620 London Regional Savings Committee 4pp *Greater London Record Office and History Library*

34621 Hornsey Parochial Charities 14pp *Greater London Record Office and History Library*

34622 Great Western (London) Housing Association Ltd 13pp *Greater London Record Office and History Library*

34623 National Amateur Rowing Association 10pp *Greater London Record Office and History Library*

34624 James Pain, architect: Irish church drawings 35pp *Representative Church Body Library*

34625 Andrew Brown Donaldson, painter: diaries and family corresp 5pp *Greater London Record Office and History Library*

34626 Joseph Welland, architect: Irish church drawings 18pp *Representative Church Body Library*

34627 Merton and Morden Historical Society 1p *Surrey Record Office*

34628 Francis John Worsley Roughton, physiologist: corresp and papers 19pp *American Philosophical Society Library*

34629 Bramley: Thorncombe Hospital Fund 3pp *Surrey Record Office, Guildford Muniment Room*

34630 Surrey Association of Trades Councils 2pp *Surrey Record Office, Guildford Muniment Room*

34631 William Denis Johnston, broadcaster: corresp and papers 26pp *Dublin University: Trinity College*

*34632 John Alan Gulland, fisheries ecologist: corresp and papers 55pp *London University: Imperial College*

34633 Sir Frederic James Osborn, town planner: corresp and papers[1] 138pp *Welwyn Garden City Central Library*

34634 Harper Garside, insurance brokers, Elland 4pp *West Yorkshire Archive Service, Calderdale*

34635 Filtrate Ltd, motor oil mfrs, Leeds 1p *West Yorkshire Archive Service, Leeds*

34636 William Williams, 'Gwilym Cyfeiliog', of Bontdolgadfan: family corresp and papers 58pp *National Library of Wales, Department of Manuscripts and Records*

34637 Philipps family of Cwmgwili: estate papers incl Jenkins family of Cilbronnau 217pp *National Library of Wales, Department of Manuscripts and Records*

34638 Nevill, Druce & Co, copper smelters, Llanelli 320pp *National Library of Wales, Department of Manuscripts and Records*

34639 Tipton Borough 18pp *Sandwell District Libraries*

34640 Wednesbury Borough 10pp *Sandwell District Libraries*

34641 Addenbrooke & Co, colliery proprietors, Tipton 8pp *Sandwell District Libraries*

34642 Williams family of Aberpergwm: family and estate papers 260pp *National Library of Wales, Department of Manuscripts and Records*

34643 Samuel Lees: corresp and papers rel to West Midlands Methodism 17pp *Sandwell District Libraries*

34644 Adam Clarke, theologian: collected letters and papers 87pp *Manchester University: Methodist Archives and Research Centre*

34645 South East Cornwall Unionist Association 1p *Cornwall Record Office*

34646 J Clarke, architect and surveyor, Liverpool 6pp *Merseyside Record Office*

34647 Arthur Ivor Pryce, solicitor and Bangor antiquary: papers 123pp *National Library of Wales, Department of Manuscripts and Records*

34648 Lewes family of Llysnewydd: family and estate papers 101pp *National Library of Wales, Department of Manuscripts and Records*

34649 Ifor Owain Wynn Williams of Bronwylfa: deeds and papers 71pp *National Library of Wales, Department of Manuscripts and Records*

34650 Helen E Behrens, genealogist: MS collection 77pp *National Library of Wales, Department of Manuscripts and Records*

---

[1]Angela Eserin and Mike Hughes: *The Sir Frederic Osborn Archive a Descriptive Catalogue*, 1990

34651 Anglesey County Council 21pp *Gwynedd Archives and Museums Service, Llangefni Area Record Office*

34652 Pembrokeshire Methodist records 23pp *Dyfed Archives Service, Pembrokeshire Area Record Office*

34653 Norfolk valuation lists 8pp *Norfolk Record Office*

34654 EN Humphreys: papers rel to Holywell-Halkyn Mining & Tunnel Co 6pp *Clwyd Record Office, Hawarden Branch*

34655 Graves Hamilton family of Mickleton: deeds and papers 49pp *Gloucestershire Record Office*

34656 Gethin family of Cernioge: deeds and estate papers 73pp *National Library of Wales, Department of Manuscripts and Records*

34657 Sheen manor records 23pp *County Record Office, Cambridge*

34658 Richards family of Caerynwch and Edwards family of Cerrigllwydion: family and estate papers 83pp *National Library of Wales, Department of Manuscripts and Records*

34659 RK Lucas & Son, estate agents, Haverfordwest: clients papers 318pp *National Library of Wales, Department of Manuscripts and Records*

34660 De Rutzen family, Barons de Rutzen, of Slebech: deeds and papers incl those of Barlow and Phillips families 322pp *National Library of Wales, Department of Manuscripts and Records*

34661 Sunderland: Humbledon Methodist Church 4pp *Tyne and Wear Archives Service*

34662 Newcastle upon Tyne: Company of Colliers, Paviors and Carriagemen 2pp *Tyne and Wear Archives Service*

34663 Association of Jewish Ex-Servicemen and Women: Newcastle upon Tyne branch 5pp *Tyne and Wear Archives Service*

34664 Staunton-on-Wye: Jarvis Charity 24pp *Hereford Record Office*

34665 Hebden Royd Urban District Council 23pp *West Yorkshire Archive Service, Calderdale*

34666 William Edleston Ltd, woollen mfrs, Sowerby Bridge 7pp *West Yorkshire Archive Service, Calderdale*

34667 Newburn Urban District Council 71pp *Tyne and Wear Archives Service*

34668 Sunderland: Park Road United Methodist Circuit 1p *Tyne and Wear Archives Service*

34669 Jarrow: Grange Road Baptist Church 9pp *Tyne and Wear Archives Service*

34670 Sunderland Mission Circuit 11pp *Tyne and Wear Archives Service*

34671 Sunderland: St Johns Methodist Church, Ashbrooke 1p *Tyne and Wear Archives Service*

34672 Scriven Crosthwaite Ltd, machine tool mfrs, Leeds 3pp *West Yorkshire Archive Service, Leeds*

34673 Walker & Smith (Batley) Ltd, textile machinery mfrs 2pp *West Yorkshire Archive Service, Leeds*

34674 Cambridge University appointments boards 60pp *Cambridge University Archives*

34675 Cambridge University: Cavendish Laboratory 21pp *Cambridge University Archives*

34676 Cambridge University: Wellingborough University Extension Society 14pp *Cambridge University Archives*

34677 Cambridge University Botanic Garden 100pp *Cambridge University Archives*

34678 British Film Institute: MS collections 275pp *British Film Institute*

34679 Horsehay Co Ltd, ironfounders, bridge builders and constructional engineers, Horsehay 1p *Ironbridge Gorge Museum Library and Archives*

34680 Sunderland: St Davids Methodist Church, Farringdon 3pp *Tyne and Wear Archives Service*

34681 Sunderland: Malings Rigg Primitive Methodist Church 1p *Tyne and Wear Archives Service*

34682 Yorkshire Cotton Operatives' Association 14pp *West Yorkshire Archive Service, Calderdale*

34683 Harold T Elwes: Welsh deeds and papers 420pp *National Library of Wales, Department of Manuscripts and Records*

34684 Sir Arthur Thomas Quiller-Couch, author and editor: corresp and papers 24pp *Oxford University: Trinity College Archives*

34685 Federation of Synagogues 47pp *Greater London Record Office and History Library*

34686 Company of the Merchants of the Staple of England 3pp *York University: Borthwick Institute of Historical Research*

34687 Lancashire and Cheshire Association for the Abolition of the State Regulation of Vice 5pp *Fawcett Library*

34688 Status of Women Committee 4pp *Fawcett Library*

34689 Womens University Settlement 30pp *Fawcett Library*

Principal replacements of and additions to existing reports included:

5279 Knollys family, Earls of Banbury: corresp and papers 219pp *Hampshire Record Office*

6494 Lawley family of Escrick, Barons Wenlock: family and estate papers 130pp *Hull University Library, Brynmor Jones Library*

10542 Innes-Ker family, Dukes of Roxburghe: family and estate papers 293pp *Private*

10737 Kerr family, Marquesses of Lothian: family and Scottish estate papers 135pp *Scottish Record Office*

10977 Macdonald family, Barons Macdonald: family and estate papers 1152pp *Private*

10979 Hamilton family, Dukes of Hamilton: family and estate papers 415pp *Scottish Record Office and Private*

12278 Sir Cuthbert Morley Headlam, MP: corresp and papers 172pp *Durham County Record Office*

12911 Wentworth family of Woolley: family and estate papers 350pp *West Yorkshire Archive Service, Yorkshire Archaeological Society*

14174 Gladstone family, baronets, of Hawarden and Glynne family, baronets: corresp and papers 270pp *St Deniols Library, Hawarden*

14609 Boulton & Watt, steam engine builders, Smethwick 448pp *Birmingham Central Library, Archives Section*

14654 Carron Co, ironfounders, engineers, coalmasters and shipowners 300pp *Scottish Record Office*

15459 Crichton-Stuart family, Marquesses of Bute: family and estate papers 95pp *Private*

15600 Worsley family, baronets, of Hovingham: family and estate papers 250pp *Private*

16471 Sir John Herbert Lewis MP: corresp and papers 188pp *National Library of Wales, Department of Manuscripts and Records*

16601 Wynn family, Barons Newborough: family and estate papers 564pp *Gwynedd Archives and Museums Service, Caernarfon Area Record Office*

18882 Alexander Mather & Son Ltd, engineers, Edinburgh 170pp *Scottish Record Office*

21847 Parsons Peebles Ltd, manufacturing electrical engineers, Edinburgh 600pp *Scottish Record Office and Private*

21856 Leigh family, Barons Leigh: family and estate papers 900pp *Shakespeare Birthplace Trust Records Office*

31601 Campbell family, Earls and Marquesses of Breadalbane: family and estate papers 700pp *Scottish Record Office*

Index to Repositories in Part I